The Rehearsal of Misunderstanding

WESLEYAN POETRY

The Rehearsal
of Misunderstanding

Three Collections
by Contemporary Greek Women Poets

BILINGUAL EDITION

§

The Cake by Rhea Galanaki
Tales of the Deep by Jenny Mastoraki
Hers by Maria Laina

§

TRANSLATED AND WITH AN INTRODUCTION

BY KAREN VAN DYCK

Wesleyan University Press
Published by University Press of New England
Hanover and London

Wesleyan University Press

University Press of New England, Hanover, NH 03755

© 1998 by Karen Van Dyck

All rights reserved

Printed in the United States of America

5 4 3 2 1

CIP data appear at the end of the book

The Greek texts of Rhea Galanaki's Το κέικ [*The Cake*] (Kedros, 1980) and
Jenny Mastoraki's Ιστορίες για τα βαθιά [*Tales of the Deep*] (Kedros, 1983)
are reproduced here by permission of Kedros Publishers. The Greek text of
Maria Laina's Δικό της [*Hers*] (Keimena, 1985) is reproduced here by per-
mission of Vaso Kyriazakou. The authors have kindly granted permission
for this translation of their work.

Publication of this book was made possible in part by funding from the
Greek Ministry of Culture.

For Jenny, Maria, and Rhea

and translate more than translate the authority,

show the choice and make no more mistakes than yesterday

Gertrude Stein, *Tender Buttons*

CONTENTS

Hers
by Maria Laina (1985)

A C K N O W L E D G M E N T S

This translation has been made possible by a grant from the National Endowment for the Arts. Subvention funds from the Greek Ministry of Culture enabled the *en face* edition. I also wish to thank Margaret Alexiou, Marilyn Katz, Dean Kostos, Mary Ann McGrail, Andrew Szegedy-Maszak, Rosanna Warren, and Marion Wilson for providing forums for presenting this material; Dimitri Gondicas and Alexander Nehamas for their support of the project; Olga Broumas, Rachel Hadas, Edmund Keeley, Gregory Sifakis, Clair Wills, and Elisabeth Young-Bruehl for their comments on the Introduction; and Katerina Anghelaki-Rooke, Kay Cicellis, Rhea Galanaki, Stathis Gourgouris, Maria Laina, Jenny Mastoraki, and Nelson Moe for their collaboration on the translations.

October 1997   K.V.D.

INTRODUCTION

At the end of Jenny Mastoraki's macabre *Tales of the Deep*, a collection of poetry full of murder, abduction, and misunderstanding, the reader finds "What that Missive Said," which purports to contain the contents of a letter. But instead of offering some long-awaited clarification, this poem warns us not to trust anyone, not even the person who is speaking. He may be a murderer or thief. The strangest twist, though, comes in the final lines which ask us to feel sympathy for the culprit.

> But when someone talks to you with terror, with voices of those lost in ghastly caves and marshes—
>
> above all you must consider what he might mean, what dismembered corpse he is hiding in his cellar, what biting kisses, murders, muffled nights, crossed noiselessly by trains (darkened by heavy curtains, with rags and cotton round the wheels), what iniquitous desires, rage, murmuring, howls, fireworks by the patrons' tombs, avengers who soak him in blood while he sleeps, what thief, finally, in a deep, brass bedchamber, smothered in linen, and cries—
>
> and you must feel for him, above all feel for him, my dear Arthur or Alphonse. (143)

Not only do we never read the real letter, but the poem suggests that no *real* letter can exist. The missive is missing. Nothing is what it seems to be, not the murderer or the murdered, not the writer or the reader. The plea to *Arthur* or

*Alph*onse is an invitation to go back to the beginning, to the *alpha*, and write the letter ourselves. Authorship, authority, and authoritativeness are all mixed up.

I begin with this unsatisfying conclusion to Mastoraki's *Tales of the Deep* because it introduces contemporary Greek women poets' recent preoccupation with misunderstanding, not only as an issue for the poet, but for any reader, critic, or translator who reads this poetry. The task of considering "what he might mean, what dismembered corpse he is hiding in his cellar" belongs to anyone who picks up this poetry. My title, *The Rehearsal of Misunderstanding*, refers to the proliferation of double entendres, obscure references, and indirect constructions in Rhea Galanaki's *The Cake*, Jenny Mastoraki's *Tales of the Deep*, and Maria Laina's *Hers,* as well as more generally to the challenges facing writers in Greece under and after the dictatorship (1967–1974). My title, however, also refers to the rehearsal of misunderstanding prompted by my translation of this poetry.

Authors under Authoritarianism

Rhea Galanaki, Jenny Mastoraki, and Maria Laina were all students at the University of Athens on April 21, 1967, when a group of junior officers took control of Greece, defeating in one effort the senior army officers, the electorate, and then the king. The colonels, as the junior officers were called, imposed strict disciplinary measures: incarcerating leftists and enforcing curfews, dress codes, and press laws. The colonels' call for order, clarity, and cleanliness had a popular appeal, and at first only a small percentage of the Greek population mobilized against the authoritarian regime. It was after the economic downturn of 1973 that growing numbers began to express their opposition in public; after the tragic events of the Polytechnic in November of the same year, when the colonels' tanks killed thirty students, national and international forces rallied and succeeded in restoring democracy.

There was, however, one form of resistance that played a central role from the beginning of the dictatorship and had a special significance both for Greek society at large and for the colonels themselves: the resistance of writers to censorship. The general public, while less aware of the torture and imprisonment that the colonels inflicted, were immediately conscious of censorship. One of the regime's first legislative actions, for example, was to stipulate that *katharevousa*, the official, "purist" language of constitutions and laws since 1911, would now also be the language of state and education. Although students were used to writing *katharevousa*, tolerance of the demotic language in schools during the 1960s had been increasing. After the coup this trend was abruptly halted and the use of *katharevousa* rigidly enforced. Unquestioned rights such as the free distribution of books or even the layout of newspapers could no longer be taken for granted. The Book Index, for example, banned not only those titles that openly criticized the regime but those whose authors' names sounded vaguely Russian, and even ancient texts that parodied the misuse of power, for example, Aristophanes' *Birds*. In one infamous case, a poet was hauled into the police station for his "communist leanings" because he had written a poem in which his lover's lips were "red."

Writers from early on set about uncovering the contradictions and hypocrisy that the regime was busy concealing. They would pretend to cooperate with the regime's mandates, only to subvert the whole project. This was evidently one reason for titling the first resistance anthology *Eighteen Texts* (1970); if, as the Press Law dictated, all books had to have titles that corresponded exactly to the contents, then the resistance would use empty titles such as *Eighteen Texts*,

6 *Poets*, *New Texts*, and *New Texts 2*. Editors of certain newspapers were known to print the regime's mandatory statements in the same type and format as obituaries. A headline in huge wood type that read "The dictatorship is rapidly receding . . . ." followed by the words "in Spain" in small type performed a trenchant social commentary.

It is in the context of a regime which tried to suppress such linguistic confusion and a literary establishment which for the most part worked to expose it that Rhea Galanaki, Jenny Mastoraki, Maria Laina, and a whole generation of younger poets first began publishing their poetry. While their elders—established poets such as the Nobel Laureate George Seferis and well-known leftist poets of the postwar generation such as Manolis Anagnostakis—for the most part returned to their previous poetic practices after censorship was lifted, for many younger poets (particularly the women), silence and hermeticism became the ground zero of expression, not a passing inconvenience. The epigrammatic poems in Galanaki's first two collections are almost impenetrable to the uninitiated. Laina's poems, though more lyrical and expressive, have a similar reined-in feeling to them. From her book *Tolls* on, Mastoraki asks at what expense one gets past censors and other kinds of toll-collectors. Censorship and the inability to say what one means is a recurring issue in their poetry.

When the colonels' regime fell in 1974 these women continued to deploy writing strategies that, although initiated in response to censorship, proved useful in articulating other power struggles. For Galanaki, Mastoraki, and Laina, the challenge to authority became a feminist problem in the late 1970s and early 1980s. Drawing on the formative experience of writing under an authoritarian regime, these women forged a poetics that established a gendered relation to censorship. The tactics for stabilizing signification upon which censorship relied were redeployed in their collections to un-settle and disrupt fixed meanings and sex roles. Writing as a woman developed, for them, out of writing under censor-ship. Unlike Lefteris Poulios and Vassilis Steriadis, two inno-vative young poets who baptized their generation "The Gen-eration of the 1970s" and initiated influential poetic trends, these women did not discard the formal training that censor-ship provided.

The politicizing of American Beat writing in Greek poetry during the 1970s and 1980s provides one striking example of where certain male and female poets of this generation parted ways. While Poulios and Steriadis completely em-braced the freedom associated with Beat writing, drawing on its use of obscenity to challenge the colonels' regime's "Greece for Christian Greeks," Galanaki's *The Cake*, eq-ually sexually explicit, also explores the less liberatory side of Ginsberg's "Howl" or Kerouac's *On the Road*. In her col-lection the man takes off on his motorcycle, but his freedom depends on a woman at home. Similarly, in a nod to the new international net of references deployed by her generation, she uses the foreign word "cake" for her title, not the tradi-tional Greek words τούρτα or γλυκό, but then goes one step further and turns this into a feminist issue by pointing out who bakes the cake.

Perhaps most significantly, though, the use of cinemato-graphic sequences of images, which typifies this generation of poets, becomes in these women's hands a feminist narra-tive poetics. As far as Galanaki, Mastoraki, and Laina are concerned, poetry should not transend linguistic and sexual confusion in a single poem's lyrical escape; instead it must partake of and participate in the confusion over the course of a longer series of poems. The sustained rehearsal of misun-derstanding in their collections functions as a feminist ploy which enables them to take up more time and space in their writing. By connecting one poem to another through repeated images and postponing resolution, a place is opened up. This is no easy task—as Laina points out, "Besides in this narrative / the difficulty / of finding a space is clear" (261). Each collection, nonetheless, manages to create a kind of typographic "room of one's own" between the covers of the book. In the 1980s women poets of this generation, as well as prominent women poets of earlier generations such as Eleni Vakalo, Kiki Dimoula, and Katerina Anghelaki-Rooke, developed strategies initiated under censorship for feminism.

Toward an unauthoritative poetry

The collections I have chosen are significant to the rise of women's writing in Greece as well as being pivotal works in the careers of each poet. Born in Crete in 1947, Galanaki began as a poet but has emerged in the past decade as one of Greece's most highly acclaimed novelists. The collection *The Cake* (1980) registers this shift from poetry to prose, forming a bridge between her early epigrammatic poems, *Albeit Pleasing* (1975) and *Minerals* (1979), and her first prose works, *Where does the Wolf Live?* (1982), *Concentric Stories* (1986), and her noted historical novels *The Life of Ismail Ferik Pasha* (1989) and *I Shall Sign My Name as Louis* (1992). *The Cake* is the most explicitly feminist text by Galanaki to date.

Mastoraki's *Tales of the Deep* similarly represents a move toward longer prose poems and women's issues. Born in Athens in 1949, Mastoraki is regarded as one of Greece's leading poets and translators. With each collection Mastoraki has written, misunderstanding has progressively become a more private affair and women's experiences have figured more and more prominently. Her book *Tolls* (1972) is explicitly about the difficulty of writing under censorship and the ways in which history and myth, from ancient to modern times, shape poetry. Her next collection of poems, *Kin* (1979), takes up similar issues with respect to personal history and myth, family genealogy, and feminine sexuality. Her last two books, *Tales of the Deep* (1983) and *With a Crown of Light* (1989), deal almost exclusively with the sufferings of those cut off from their histories, communities, and families: self-absorbed lovers, abandoned children, fugitives. In *Tales of the Deep*, particularly, what one can and cannot say is a feminist matter.

Laina's *Hers* also opens a window on the relations among misunderstanding, gender, and narrative poetry in the 1980s. Born in 1947 in Patras, Maria Laina is widely regarded as one of the best writers of her generation. Since the mid-1980s she has also been writing for the theater. Her most recent collection of poetry, *Rose Colored Fear* (1992), received the National Prize for Poetry. The central problem throughout Laina's poetry is how to come to grips with a look that censors her by not recognizing her, how to describe a kind of love that others do not understand. While Galanaki and Mastoraki define feminine sexuality in relation to the opposite sex, Laina hardly ever mentions men. The love she wants to describe, at times lesbian, at other times, auto-erotic, is never socially acceptable. The project of clearing a space for such a kind of love is charted over the course of her earlier volumes: *Beyond* (1970), *Change of Scene* (1972), *Punctuation Marks* (1979). But it is in *Hers* that narrative and women's issues intersect in the typographic project of finding a place on the page.

How do these collections create a tentative space for women's writing? To what extent does women's writing undermine authority by positing misunderstanding and misrepresentation as constitutive of meaning? While the language and vision of each poet is obviously distinct, these collections reveal certain affinities in the way they provide responses to such questions. Rhea Galanaki's *The Cake* follows a pregnant woman through her day as she weighs the ingredients for a cake. The cake in the process of being baked stands in for the as-yet-unborn son (the etymology of placenta derives from the ancient Greek πλακούς, "a flat cake"), and suggests that any act of definition that represents something intact and finished is flawed. As one poem puts it: "The definition's clothing is the same as its wording and both are torn to shreds" (53). The impossibility of a word representing a definition, of a cake symbolizing a child, produces the endless deferral and fraying that is the text the reader holds in her hands. Galanaki calls this kind of language feminine. Unlike masculine language, it does not "close like a lake," but instead "wells up" like a spring (77), constantly in motion, making and unmaking itself.

Mastoraki's *Tales of the Deep* also suggests that women's writing is different, less static than the established male mode of writing. In one devastating poem she reveals the violence men's euphemisms conceal:

> "My fair ones!" they would call them as they cornered them. Later they turned them into songs. Exemplary ladies. With bruised necks. Crumpled petticoats. And on their linen pantalets, a stain of blood, a dark leaf, spreading.
>
> Let that be what is left of ancient longings. And of ancient loves. (89)

While the masculine language of seductive banter and bragging songs entraps, feminine language appears to be more like the spreading blood, without distinct boundaries. Over the course of Mastoraki's collection, the bruises, stains, and cracks become the figures of a new language that, like a mirror in a funhouse, deforms and exaggerates rather than imitates clearly. In another poem even a reflection in still water registers a dismembered body and text: "the domes covered over with flying corpses, dislocated bones, and awful fractures, postures of extreme agony . . ." (123).

Laina's collection also insists on rehearsing in language the effect of being misunderstood and misrepresented. *Hers* starts, for example, with the poem "Fresco," which parodies a masculine archaeological report for attempting to salvage the image of a woman, for trying to make her whole again.

> The beginning of the thighs still remains
> a dull blue
> to the left a section of foot unadorned
> and a section from the hem of the dress. (147)

The poem continues in this descriptive vein. The final line, though, is set off typographically and initiates a different, less technical, more conversational tone, one that characterizes the rest of the collection: "The ground of love is missing" (147). The implied archaeologist is looking for the wrong thing. Even if he were to succeed in putting the woman back together again, something else would still be missing. The protagonist of the poems, Maria—the author's name, but also the most common Greek name for women— then proceeds to sit down in front of a mirror and try to find a place of her own, "hers," as the collection's title suggests, where she can be fragmented but not lacking, where she can live as one poem puts it, "without elbows / or knees" (227).

Each of the three collections included in this anthology works out the myriad ways we are misunderstood and misrepresented by others and ourselves. Like recent American language poetry by women that draws on the work of Emily Dickinson and Gertrude Stein, these series of interwoven poems transform hermeticism into a feminine survival strategy for recognizing how meaning is lost, disfigured, or denied. They put off resolution indefinitely by making that which is missing an integral part of their content and form. Their rehearsal of misunderstanding challenges authorship, authority, and authoritativeness by suggesting that control over others and ourselves is an illusion. At the very moment of consolidation, of checking one's reflection in still water or in a mirror, the body is found in pieces. Nothing is what it purports to be. Representation is fundamentally misrepresentation.

An Autobiography of Translation

Having placed these women poets and their poetics in the political and literary context of contemporary Greece, let me turn to the implications of their project for translation, and in particular for my translation of their poetry. A first question suggests itself: If the original is not intact, a "whole," but makes what is missing a part of its structural content, how does this ellipsis affect the translator's usual goal of reconstruction? A second question follows: How might this poetry suggest a translation practice that acknowledges its own distortion, fragmentation, exaggeration, attenuation, misrepresentation, and misunderstanding? The questions are provocative in theory, but what about in practice? To illustrate the rehearsal of misunderstanding that translation also involves, let me offer an autobiography of my translation of Mastoraki's *Tales of the Deep*.

In working with Mastoraki's text, as well as Galanaki's and Laina's, I was impressed by this poetry's visual impact. In the Greek literary context where the oral tradition of the folksong is so prized, these collections were all about physical, visually present, written texts, particularly from Byzantium on. Mastoraki's *Tales of the Deep*, for example, progressively privileges the written over the oral, moving from the performative language of folktales, stage directions, and spells to a metatextual meditation on narrative and irreparable manuscripts. This progression from orality to textuality is supported formally by techniques akin to collage and montage. The poet pastes more and more bits of different texts—lines from Greece's national poet Dionysios Solomos, translations of Victorian idylls, Jules Verne's adventure tales, Byzantine chronicles—in closer and closer proximity so that in the second half of *Tales of the Deep*, poems become dense, even palimpsestic, with words and images piled one on top of the other. Repeated references, for example, to walls and wounds visually connect unrelated scenes cinematographically, functioning much the way meter and rhyme might in more traditional poetry.

In the beginning, my translation, not altogether consciously, foregrounded the visual impact of Mastoraki's poems. I made sure repeated words in Greek were translated consistently, even if two different words might have worked better in English. My purpose was to show how words function for Mastoraki as images, reproducing different historical moments through the look of their spelling, accents, and breathing marks. (Her insistence on the polytonic system of accents over the now more accepted monotonic system reflects this.) I tried to create the peculiarly visual appeal of Mastoraki's use of so many different linguistic registers by including archaic, quaint phrases such as "ablaze" and "brazzera," emphasizing how certain words or phrases recall the language of other times. I made choices based on my critical preoccupation with the writerliness of these texts. Finally, to give the reader the full cumulative effect, I decided not to publish these poems separately in journals, but to keep them together as a long narrative series.

Eventually I sent a draft to Mastoraki to read. As she herself is one of Greece's foremost literary translators, I was particularly interested in her comments. Over the years I had been in touch with the poets whose work I planned to include in the anthology. We had met and discussed certain difficult passages early on, but I had not shown them how my translations had evolved along with my critical analysis of their poetry. When it came time to request permission to publish parts of their texts in my study of Greek poetry under and after the dictatorship, I also sent my translations. The letter I received from Mastoraki was frighteningly like the letter that was never delivered in her *Tales of the Deep*, the missing missive: she was not going to authorize my translation because it was full of misunderstandings. The final poem of *Tales of the Deep*, which warns the reader to beware the dismembered corpse buried in the writer's meaning, suddenly seemed oddly prophetic. The border between life and literature became blurred.

While her poetry resisted closure by deferring the arrival of the letter, by inverting murderer and murdered, writer and reader, the author was understandably less willing to relinquish authority when the issue was the translation of her poetry. Though my first response was to ask how she, who had invited me into the text's multiple meanings, could turn and attempt to restrict its meaning, I then thought about the way she had criticized me: buried in the logic of her letter were important lessons about the politics of translation.

Over the years as a student and translator of this Greek cultural scene I had gained a certain status, a certain authority: I had published in scholarly journals; I had a job at a university. Around the same time that Mastoraki's letter was written, my work on her poetry was cited in a Greek Sunday newspaper. I saw my name in English in the midst of Greek print and recognized myself for the first time as the foreigner in that centuries-old game in which one looks for approval to an outsider. This is a game that has a particular painful history in Greece where no generation has been unscathed by foreign intervention (American, British, French, German, Turkish). On the one hand the mention was flattering; on the other, it was disconcerting. I did not want to admit I was the foreigner my name inscribed me to be. I was attached to my adopted Greek identity—all those years of being told "είσαι δικιά μας" (you are one of us) and "μιλάς καλύτερα από μας" (you speak better than we do). I hadn't understood how my own authority with regard to Greek culture relied on both my status as a foreigner and on my adopted Greek identity, both on being an outsider and on being an insider.

Mastoraki's mode of questioning my authority rewrote these positions. First she uncovered the imperialist overtones of my authority as a foreigner, by asserting that as a foreigner I did not understand Greek and never truly could. Then she used my familiarity with Greece, my status as an insider, to discipline me. She read into my own definition of myself as foreign authority and as adopted daughter the cultural legacy of both these positions. Mastoraki's letter made me realize that if I claimed to be both outsider and insider, I had to recognize my complicity in the patriotic and patriarchal narratives that say that foreigners must be deferred to and that daughters must be disciplined. This realization did not render my translation worthless; it simply applied pressure, a pressure that made me accountable as an author and as an authority for my authoritativeness even when I most wanted to cede it. As Mastoraki suggests in *Tales of the Deep*, one always identifies the corpse hidden in the cellar, just as the endless undecidability of meaning is being flaunted. The lesson being perhaps not *only* to go back and write the *Tales* ourselves, but also to accept that as translators we are always also murderers, thieves, distorters, and mutilaters, to find ways to acknowledge the parts of our narratives that disable us, as well as those that enable us.

When I arrived in Greece to work on the translation with Mastoraki it turned out there were very few linguistic mistakes. My knowledge of Greek was not the issue. Her real criticism of my translation was my lack of attention to the rhythm. It seems that my concern for the visual impact of her poetry, its textuality, had meant that I had neglected this more traditionally lauded ingredient of Greek poetry. I had taken the unauthoritativeness of her poetry to an extreme. I had concentrated on her visual poetics at the expense of the orality of her text. By fixating on what was novel about her poetics, I had eliminated the struggle between orality and visuality. She explained how the poems relied on an oral and visual contradiction, the gentle rhythmic lilt contrasting with the cruel, visual images of rape, abduction, and drowning.

Collaboration turned out to be crucial for destabilizing authorship and authority. Seated across from each other in various *tavernas* and *kafeneions* neither of us could take full control. She would hammer the rhythm of each poem into my head until I found an appropriate equivalent in English and then I would turn and say "but now this word, this image, this gesture is lost, what do we do?" We were able to keep each other aware of when either of us tried too hard to push our critical agendas: Mastoraki's view was that her text was a part of the Greek literary canon and oral tradition, while I wanted to show its feminist break with that tradition. Collaboration, whether with the author, another poet, another critic, or with oneself over time, is a way of owning up to how translation depends as much on misunderstanding as it does on understanding.

The autobiography I have just elaborated in some way outlines a less authoritative approach to translation. Autobiography provides a mode for making explicit one's reasons for representing another language and culture, for speaking for someone else. Contextualized, authority becomes less definitive and the need for different perspectives becomes more evident. But this autobiographical mode also has certain drawbacks, especially in the context of the kind of poetry I am introducing. Autobiography in its many different generic permutations—memoirs, confession, personal criticism—most often assumes that life can be represented in a narrative sequence and that the person writing is the sum of all that has been recounted. Autobiography inevitably offers relief: "Oh, that's the reason she did that." "Oh, I understand now." The autobiography here is no exception. Even though I have tried to decenter it by calling it an autobiography of translation, not of me personally, my account, nevertheless, relies on the resolution autobiography promises. Fundamentally the autobiography of translation can only go so far in destabilizing the translator's authority.

The translations, however, as poetry, offer other modes for thinking about issues of authority and authoritativeness. As we have seen, both the message and the medium of these collections undermine the feasibility of any resolution or clearly identifiable subject. Rather than insisting on clarification and self-knowledge, this poetry rehearses the misunderstandings that impede such projects. The writing self, instead of being the origin of meaning, is the scene of a violent dissolution. As a line from Mastoraki's *Tales of the Deep* illustrates: "so they resemble you, torn to shreds, and you them, again, in pieces" (91). Or as Laina's collection *Hers* concludes "And me, what do I know? What do I know?" (285). This poetry asks, What kind of an autobiography is possible if the "auto" (self) is always on the move, adopting different stances, plural and in pieces?

In each of the three translations that follow, the rehearsal of misunderstanding becomes a critique of the resolution and stable subject-position my autobiography of translation constructs. By ending with the poetry itself, I can leave the letter undelivered and prompt you to go back to the beginning and write the tales yourselves, thus offering the possibility of new readings and translations, rather than authorizing mine.

The Rehearsal of Misunderstanding

ΡΕΑ ΓΑΛΑΝΑΚΗ

τό κέικ

ΚΕΔΡΟΣ

Τοῦ Ἠλία

The Cake

by Rhea Galanaki

For Elias

Α΄

Τό ἕνα καί τό ἄλλο μέτρο

I

One and the Other Kind of Measure

1. Κρατᾶς τή ζυγαριά τῆς ἡδονῆς μ' ὅλους τούς δίσκους. Γέρνει ὅπου κάθε φορά βαραίνει ὁ σφαγμένος κόκορας. Σφαγμένος καί χτυπώντας τά φτερά καί πιτσιλώντας αἷμα σκαρφαλώνει στό διπλό κρεβάτι γιά νά ξεψυχήσει ἐπάνω στά λευκά σεντόνια σου κι ἐσύ, ἐσύ ἀγγίζεις αἷμα στά φορέματα σά νά γεννᾶς· ἀγγίζεις αἷμα στό μαντίλι πού ἔχεις δέσει γύρω ἀπό τά μάτια σου σά νά μποροῦσες νά ζυγίζεις ἀμερόληπτα· τό αἷμα σου ἀγγίζεις.

Γέρνει ὁ δίσκος πού βαραίνεις μέ τό δικό σου δάχτυλο καί τή σκιά τοῦ κόκορα· ἀκίνητη γιγαντιαία σ' ἕνα τοῖχο ἡ σκιά του καί κοντά στό φῶς τά δάχτυλά σου ἀκίνητα μπλεγμένα. Βαραίνεις μέ τό σφαγμένο δάχτυλο καί πιτσιλᾶ τό αἷμα στό τραπέζι τῆς κουζίνας, ὅπου ζυγίζεις πόσο ἀλεύρι, πόση ζάχαρη καί πόσο βούτυρο γιά μιάν ἐπέτειο· τό σῶμα σου μέσ' στό καλό του φόρεμα ζυγίζει, μέσα στό φόρεμα γιγαντιαία καί ἀκίνητη κρατώντας, εἶναι σάν ἤδη νά κρατᾶς στά χέρια σου τό κέικ.

1. You hold the scales of pleasure with all the trays. The scale tips each time the slaughtered cock weighs it down. Slaughtered and beating its wings and splattering blood it clambers onto the double bed to die on your white sheets and you, you touch the bloody clothes as if you were giving birth; you touch the bloody kerchief you tied over your eyes as if you could weigh things impartially; you touch your blood.

The tray tips when you push down with your finger and the shadow of the cock; gigantic and immobile, his shadow on the wall and near the light your fingers, folded and immobile. You push down with your slaughtered finger and it splatters blood on the kitchen table, where you weigh the right amount of flour, sugar, and butter for an anniversary; your body in its best dress is weighing, in its best dress gigantic, immobile, it is holding, it is as if you were already holding the cake in your hands.

2. Μέσα στ' ἀκίνητο γιγαντιαῖο φόρεμά σου νά βαδίζεις. Βαδίζει σ' ἕνα τοῖχο ἡ σκιά σου ὅπως ἐσύ διασχίζεις τό ταψί· ἄδειο ταψί κι ἐσύ, ἀσύλληπτη νά τό διασχίζεις ἀπό μάτι. Κανένας ἄλλος ὄγκος ἀπό τό δικό σου σῶμα καί δίχως χρώματα ἐκτός τό κόκκινο ζεστό· πού μόλις γέννησες ἤ θά γεννήσεις. Βαδίζεις ὥσπου φτάνεις στήν ἄκρη καί γυρνᾶς, φτάνεις σέ μιάν ἄλλη ἄκρη καί γυρνᾶς, φτάνεις σέ μιά τρίτη ἄκρη καί γυρνᾶς, φτάνεις γυρνᾶς. Κάθε πού σταματᾶς εἶναι καί μιά προσωπική σου ἐπέτειος. Τό σῶμα σου κινεῖται, τίποτε ἄλλο δέν κινεῖται ἀπό τό σῶμα σου σάν ἐκκρεμές κι ὁρίζεις πρίν ἀπό τόν Γαλιλαῖο. Στά χέρια σου κρατᾶς ἕνα μεγάλο κέικ κι ἀφήνεις σ' ὅλες τίς ἐπέτειους ἕνα κομμάτι σάν νά ἐγκαταλείπεις σ' ὅλες τίς παγίδες ἕνα ἴχνος ἀπό τή διάρκειά σου· μέχρι πότε;

2. Inside your gigantic, immobile dress you are walking. Your shadow is walking across the wall as you cross the pan; an empty pan, and you, difficult to grasp, move across it. There is no other mass except your body and no colors except for something hot and red; which you just gave birth to or will give birth to. You walk until you reach the edge and then turn, you reach another edge and turn, you reach a third edge and turn, you reach and turn. Each time you stop it is a personal anniversary. Your body is moving, nothing else is moving except your body like a pendulum and you define motion before Galileo. In your hands you hold a big cake and you leave a piece at every anniversary as if you were abandoning in every trap some proof of your ability to last; for how long?

3. Ὁ κυνηγός κρατᾶ σπαθί ἀντί γιά δίκαννο· ὁ κυνηγός δέ θά μποροῦσε· ὁ κυνηγός κρατώντας τό σπαθί δέ θά μποροῦσε νά 'χει ἄλλο τρόπο γιά νά ζεῖ κοντά σου ἀπό τό κυνήγι. Ὁ κυνηγός κουράζεται νά τρέχει· ἐπάνω στή μοτοσικλέτα τρέχει, στούς δρόμους τρέχει σάν μέσα στό πηγάδι τοῦ γύρου τοῦ θανάτου· κουράζεται καί ξαποσταίνει σέ μιάν ὑπαίθρια πηγή μέσα στίς φτέρες τῆς πλατείας Ὁμονοίας· ἐκεῖ τρώει ἕνα κομμάτι κέικ. Θά ἤθελε νά σταματήσει· θά ἤθελε νά σταματήσει τό κυνήγι καί νά φύγει σέ χώρα μακρινή· ὅπου ἕνα δωμάτιο ἥσυχο βρόμικο καί λίγο σκοτεινό ἀτομικό του· ὅπου δέ θά ξαναφοβηθεῖ τήν πείνα. Ἀνασαίνει βαθιά μέ κλειστά μάτια· ἀνασαίνει, ἀνοίγει τά μάτια καί βάζει τό ξυπνητήρι γιατί θά πρέπει νά σηκωθεῖ καί νά σέ κυνηγήσει κι ἀνασαίνοντας τά ξαναχλείνει. Ξέρει ἀπέξω αὐτές τίς διαδρομές, ὅπως ἀπέξω ξέρει καί τίς ἐπετείους καί τό ἐκκρεμές τῆς κίνησής σου καί τή γεύση καί δέν ἔχει· δέν ἔχει ἄλλο τρόπο γιά νά ζεῖ κοντά σου ἀπό τό κυνήγι.

3. The hunter holds a sword instead of a shotgun; the hunter has no other means, the hunter holding the sword has no other means of living near you besides hunting. The hunter gets tired of racing; racing on a motorcycle, racing through the streets as if on some death-defying roller coaster; he is tired and rests by a fountain in the ferns at Omonia Square; there he eats a piece of cake. He would like to stop; he would like to stop hunting and go to a faraway land; a room of his own, quiet, dirty, not much light; a place where he would never be hungry. He breathes deeply with his eyes closed; he breathes, opens his eyes and sets the alarm clock since he will have to get up and hunt you and he closes them again, breathing. He knows these routes by heart, just as he knows your anniversaries and your pendulum motion and the taste and he has no other means; he has no other means of living near you besides hunting.

4. Ὁ κυνηγός ἀσκεῖ ἀρχαῖο ἐπάγγελμα· σκοτώνει τούς ἀρχαίους μύθους καί τούς κρεμᾶ σ' ἕνα τσιγκέλι ἀνάποδα. Ὁ κυνηγός δέν ἔχει ἄλλο τρόπο ἀπό τό κυνήγι, δέν ἔχει ἄλλο τρόπο γιά νά ζεῖ κοντά σου κι ἀνοίγει τήν κοιλιά τους μέ τό κοφτερό σπαθί. Θά ἤθελε νά μάθει τί κάνει τόν λαγό λαγό: τά δάχτυλα μέσα στά σπλάχνα, τό σκοῦρο παγωμένο αἷμα, τά ἔντερα καί τό συκώτι κι ἡ καρδιά καί τό ἀνύπαρκτο σημεῖο σήψης κι ἡ ζέστα τῆς ζωῆς στήν τελευταία ἑτοιμόρροπη σταγόνα. Ὁ κυνηγός τραβᾶ τά χέρια του καί διαμελίζουν τό ἀνοιγμένο σῶμα. Ἀνάβουν τήν ἠλεκτρική κουζίνα. Κόβουν, γιά τό λαγό, πολλά κρεμμύδια στήν μεγάλη κατσαρόλα. Προσθέτουν δάφνη. Ὁ κυνηγός βάζει τό πιάτο στό τραπέζι τῆς κουζίνας γιά νά φάει. Θά ἤθελε νά ζεῖ, θά ἤθελε πολύ νά ζεῖ ἀπαραμύθητος κι ἐλεύθερος. Δέν ἔχει ἄλλο τρόπο γιά νά ζεῖ· νά ζεῖ κοντά σου ἀπό τό κυνήγι καί δέν μπορεῖ, δέ θά μποροῦσε νά σκοτώσει ὅλους τούς λαγούς γιατί θά μέναν δυό καί θά γεννοῦσαν ἕναν τρίτο, σάν νά σέ κουβαλᾶ καί νά σέ γονιμοποιεῖ ὁ ἴδιος ἀπ' ὅ,τι θά θυμᾶται. Ἀνελεύθερος θυμᾶται.

4. The hunter practices an ancient profession; he kills ancient myths and hangs them upside down from a meat hook. The hunter has no other means besides hunting, he has no other means of living near you and he cuts open their stomachs with his sharp sword. He would like to know what makes a hare a hare: the fingers inside the entrails, the dark congealed blood, the intestines and the liver and the heart and the absent signs of decay and the warmth of something living in the last pendulous drop. The hunter withdraws his hands tearing apart the open body. His hands switch on the electric stove, chopping many onions into a big pot for the hare, adding a bay leaf. The hunter puts the plate on the kitchen table in order to eat. He would like to live, he would so much like to live without the consolation of myth and free. He has no other means of living; of living near you besides hunting and he cannot, he could not kill all the hares since two would survive and they would give birth to a third, as if he were carrying you, impregnating you himself with all that he will remember. Unfree, he remembers.

Β′
Οἱ παγίδες

II

The Traps

5. Τό δόκανο μιᾶς ἐπετείου. Εἶπε ὁ κυνηγός τόσο ἀλεύρι, τόσο βούτυρο καί τόση ζάχαρη μοῦ φτιάχνουν ἕνα σιδερένιο κέικ.

5. An anniversary snare. The hunter said this much flour this much butter and this much sugar will make me an iron cake.

6. Όταν τοῦ χάρισες ἕνα σπαθί· ὅταν τοῦ χάρισες τόν κίνδυνο τῆς διανυχτέρευσης πάνω ἀπό μύθους πού ψυχομαχοῦν καί σοῦ ἐξομολογοῦνται τίς ἑρμηνεῖες τους καί σοῦ ζητοῦν συγχώρεση· ὅταν τοῦ χάρισες τόν κίνδυνο τοῦ ὅρκου ὅτι θά πεθάνεις ὅταν κι ἐκεῖνοι θά πεθάνουν· τόν κίνδυνο ἑνός ἀγγίγματος δαχτύλων· τόν κίνδυνο τοῦ ἐπιφωνήματος κουράγιο καί τῆς ἐπιθυμίας ἄφεσης· τόν κίνδυνο μιᾶς σωτηρίας ὁραματικῆς· ὅταν σέ εἶδε νά ζυγίζεις στήν κουζίνα.

Όταν τοῦ χάρισες ἕνα σπαθί καί σύ καθόσουνα σ' ἕνα σκαμνάκι πλάι σ' ἕνα κρεβάτι τοῦ νοσοκομείου· καί σύ καθόσουνα σ' ἕνα σκαμνάκι πλάι σ' ὅλα τά κρεβάτια τοῦ ἄσπρου λαϊκοῦ θαλάμου κι ἄκουγες τή μοτοσικλέτα νά βογκᾶ καί νά πεθαίνει· ὁ ἦχος της. Όταν τόν εἶδες ὄρθιο καί σοβαρό νά ὑπολογίζει τόσα πλευρά, τόσα ἀνοίγματα καί τό σπαθί μπηγμένο στήν καρδιά τοῦ μύθου· καί τόν εἶδες ὄρθιο σοβαρό νά βρίσκει ἀκριβῶς τή θέση τῆς ἀσθενικῆς καρδιᾶς ὅπως τό βύθιζε· ὅπως ἐβύθιζε τό βλέμμα του στά μάτια σου καί ὅπως ἄλλαζε τό βλέμμα του ὅσο βυθιζόταν. Ἐσκέφτηκες φοβᾶμαι. Αὐτόν τόν ἄσπρο θάλαμο μέ τούς ἀρρώστους. Κι εἶδες τόν κυνηγό σκουπίζοντας τά αἵματα στίς γάμπες σου καί κουμπωνόταν· ἀλλά δέν εἶχε βλέμμα. Δέν εἶχε βλέμμα ὅπως ἔφευγε νά δεῖ τό πρόσωπό του ἑτοιμοθάνατο καί ξαπλωμένο νά τό χαϊδεύεις καί νά τό παρηγορεῖς, τό πρόσωπό του σ' ὅλα τά κρεβάτια. Δέν εἶχε βλέμμα καί θά ξαναρχόταν νά σκοτώσει καί τούς ἄλλους. Ἤδη ἐσύ ριγμένη ξύλιαζες πάνω στό πρωτοριγμένη πάνω σέ δεκάδες ἄσπρα κρεβάτια ξύλιαζες.

6. When you gave him a sword; when you gave him the danger of spending the night on top of myths in the throes of death that confess their meanings and beg your forgiveness; when you gave him the danger of an oath that you would die when they die; the danger of fingers touching; the danger of a courageous exclamation, and the desire for absolution; the danger of a visionary salvation; when he saw you weighing things in the kitchen.

When you gave him a sword and you sat on a stool next to a hospital bed; and you sat on a stool next to all the beds in the white public ward and you heard the motorcycle moan and die; its sound. When you saw him standing there serious, estimating this many ribs, this many openings, and the sword buried in the heart of myth; and you saw him standing there serious, locating the exact position of the ailing heart as he sank the sword in; as he sank his eyes into yours and the way his look changed as it sank in. You thought, I am scared. That white ward with the sick people. And you saw the hunter wiping the blood on your thighs and buttoning up; but he had no way of seeing. He had no way of seeing his own face as he left, near death, laid out for you to caress and console, his face in all the hospital beds. He had no way of seeing and he would come again to kill the others too. Already shivering on top of the first bed you grew rigid; shuddering on top of all the white hospital beds you grew rigid.

Θά ξαναρχόταν καί θά ήθελε· πόσο θά ήθελε μέ τόν ήλεκτρισμό ή μ' έναν τρόπο χημικό άθόρυβο άπρόσωπο χωρίς κανένα ύγρό χωρίς κανένα στέρεο χωρίς κανένα σῶμα καί κανένα βλέμμα. Όταν ξαναρχόταν.

He would come again and it would please him; how it would please him to come through an electrical current or chemically noiseless impersonal without any fluids or solids without a body or a look. When he would come again.

7. Καί μετά τόν πρῶτο νεκρό ὁ κυνηγός· ὁ κυνηγός ἀνασαίνει βαθιά μέ κλειστά μάτια καί θά ξεκουραστεῖ. Θά χτυπήσει· τό ξυπνητήρι θά χτυπήσει. Στά ὑπόλοιπα κρεβάτια πρέπει νά σέ κυνηγήσει, γιατί κάθε κρεβάτι εἶναι μιά ἐπέτειος καί κάθε ἐπέτειος εἶναι παγίδα. Ὅπως μοσχοβολᾶ. Τότε πού σβήνει τή μοτοσικλέτα ὁ κυνηγός καί ἀνασαίνει τή μυρωδιά τοῦ κομματιοῦ· ἕνα κομμάτι ἀπό τό κέικ κι ἀνασαίνει βαθιά μέ κλειστά μάτια σά νά ξεκουράζεται πάνω σέ χνάρια κόκκινα καί σέ ἀνιχνεύει.

7. And after the first corpse the hunter; the hunter breathes deeply with his eyes closed and he will rest. It will ring; the alarm clock will ring. He must hunt for you in the rest of the beds, because each bed is an anniversary and each anniversary is a trap. The way it smells sweet. When the hunter turns off the motorcycle and breathes in the scent a piece makes; a piece of the cake and he breathes deeply with his eyes closed as if he were resting on top of red tracks and he chases you down.

8. Ὅταν γεννήσεις, γιατί πάντα θά γεννήσεις· τότε θά κάνεις ἕνα πιό μεγάλο κέικ νά μοσχοβολᾶ. Ὅταν γεννήσεις καί θά τό μοιράσεις σέ πολλά κομμάτια καί πάνω σέ κάθε κομμάτι θά ὑπάρχει ἕνα κερασάκι. Ὅταν γεννήσεις· καί γιά νά μοιράσεις τέτοιο κέικ θά χρειαστεῖς ἕνα μεγάλο· τό σπαθί πού χάρισες θά χρειαστεῖς, πού τό κρατᾶ ἐκεῖνο τό μπαλάκι τοῦ πίνγκ-πόνγκ, γιατί ἔτσι μοιάζει ὅπως τινάζεται στά ξαφνικά καί σέ ἀκολουθεῖ. Καί μοιάζει νά σέ κυνηγᾶ. Ἐδῶ πού στέκεσαι, ἕνα κομμάτι κέικ ἀχνιστό ἐδῶ, σ᾽ αὐτό τό τρίστρατο· ἕνα κομμάτι κέικ βουτηγμένο στό δικό σου αἷμα γιατί φοβᾶσαι, τή γέννα ὅπως φοβᾶσαι καί τόν κυνηγό κι ὅπως ἐσκέφτηκες τόν ἄσπρο θάλαμο μέ φόβο. Ἕνα καταφύγιο. Σάν ξόρκι. Ἡ νοσταλγία ἑνός καταφυγίου καί ἀγκαλιάζεις μέ τά δυό σου χέρια τή μεγάλη σου κοιλιά· βυθίζεσαι στή μήτρα τοῦ παλιότερου μύθου· νά σέ κυοφορήσει, ἔμβρυο πού κυοφορεῖς ἕν᾽ ἄλλο ἔμβρυο. Ἐκεῖ εὐδαίμονη σιωπή καί χαραγμένη, μόνο ἀπό τό ξερό τραγούδι τῆς μπάλας τοῦ πίνγκ-πόνγκ. Ἔρχεται κατά ᾽δῶ, ξύλινο χελιδόνι· πληγωμένο καί κάθεται στή φούχτα σου. Τό χαϊδεύεις. Τό βάζεις φύλακα στά μάγια σου. Νά ψέλνει ὥσπου νά ψοφήσει.

8. When you give birth, because you will always give birth; then you will make a bigger cake that smells sweet. When you give birth and you will divide it into many pieces and on top of each piece there will be a cherry. When you give birth; and in order to divide such a cake you will need a big; the sword you gave away, you will need, which the ping-pong ball holds, because that is what he looks like when he suddenly flies out and follows you. And he looks like he is hunting you. Here where you are standing, a piece of steaming hot cake here, at this crossroads; a piece of cake drowning in your own blood because you are afraid, of the birth the way you are afraid of the hunter and the way you thought about the white hospital ward with fear. A shelter. Like a spell. The nostalgia for a shelter and you hug your big belly with both hands; you bury yourself in the womb of the older myth; to be pregnant with you, an embryo pregnant with another embryo. Over there a blissful silence, scored only by the dry song of a ping-pong ball. It comes nearer, a wounded wooden swallow and sits in the palm of your hand. You caress it. You make it the guardian of your magic. To sing until death.

9. Ὁ κυνηγός δέν τραγουδᾶ οὔτε μιλᾶ ποτέ. Ὅταν ἡ καρδιά του χτυπᾶ ἀπό τό τρέξιμο, ἀκούγονται οἱ μηχανές ἑνός τυπογραφείου πού κάνει ὑπερωρίες. Ὅταν τρώει, ἀκούει τόσο δυνατά τά δόντια του νά ροκανίζουν, πού σταματᾶ νά τρώει καί ἀκούει. Ὅταν ξεκουράζεται στήν πηγή, σβήνει ὁ ἦχος τῆς μοτοσιχλέτας κι ἀρχίζει μιά σιγανή βροχή, μέχρι νά τή διακόψει τό ξυπνητήρι. Ὅταν σκοτώνει, ἀκούει πρῶτος τό οὐρλιαχτό τοῦ ἄλλου. Ὅταν ἀγαπᾶ, ἕνα μικρό παιδί σέρνει ἀπ' τό σπάγκο τό ξύλινο σκυλάκι μέ τίς ρόδες στήν πλάτη σου. Ὅταν κλαίει, ἀκούγεται τό ἀπίστευτο κλάμα του.

9. The hunter never sings nor speaks. When his heart beats from racing around, the printing presses can be heard working overtime. When he eats, his teeth gnaw so loudly that he stops eating to listen. When he rests at the fountain, the sound of the motorcycle stops and a gentle rain begins to fall, until the alarm clock interrupts. When he kills, he hears the howl of the other first. When he loves, a young child pulls a wooden puppy with wheels on a string up and down your back. When he cries, his unbelievable cry is heard.

10. Ἄν ἡ δική σου φαντασία εἶναι τό δόκανο, αὐτό πού ἔκρυψε σέ μιάν ἐπέτειο ὁ κυνηγός σά σιδερένιο κέικ· τότε καί τό δικό σου τό παιχνίδι παγιδεύει στήν τελετουργία του τόν κυνηγό: ὁ μικρός κυνηγός παίζει. Γιά ὧρες σκέφτεται πῶς παίζεται ἕνα παιχνίδι ὅπως ὁ μάστορας τά ὑλικά του. Ἕνα παιχνίδι μέ προκαθορισμένη συμμετρία, ἀνάμεσα σέ δυό ὁμάδες. Ἕνα παιχνίδι μ' ἕνα τυπικό ἀσύμμετρο, ἀνάμεσα σέ ζωντανούς καί σέ νεκρούς· σέ ἱερά καί κατά κόσμον· σέ ἱερουργό καί σέ πιστούς. Ἕνα παιχνίδι τελετουργικό, ὅπου νικῶ σημαίνει πῶς σκοτώνω τόν ἀντίπαλό μου. Ἕνα παιχνίδι μέ τυχαία ἔκβαση.

10. If your own imagination is the snare, the snare the hunter hid on an anniversary like an iron cake; then your game also traps the hunter in its ritual: the young hunter is playing. For hours he thinks about how a game is played the way a builder thinks about his materials. A game with predetermined symmetry, between two teams. A game with an assymmetrical rite, between the living and the dead; between sacred and secular; between celebrant and believers. A ritualistic game, where winning means I kill my opponent. A game with a chance outcome.

Γ'
Τό παιχνίδι

III

The Game

11. Ἀργό παιχνίδι.

Τό πληγωμένο φίδι δίνει τόν ρυθμό τοῦ παιχνιδιοῦ καί τό παιχνίδι θά μποροῦσε νά ὀνομαστεῖ «τό πληγωμένο φίδι». Κανένας ἦχος, ὅπως δέν ὑπάρχει πικρή μπουκιά στό κέικ: φρέσκια πληγή στό φίδι νά αἱμορραγεῖ, βουβή ἀετίνα πού τό κυνηγᾶ νά τό σκοτώσει, θάμνοι πού ἴσως θά τό σώσουν.

Τό πληγωμένο φίδι δίνει τόν ρυθμό τοῦ παιχνιδιοῦ. Ἡ ἀετίνα δέν πρέπει νά κινεῖται γρηγορότερα· ἡ ἀγωνία τῶν ἐκφραστικῶν κινήσεων: μιά σύσπαση τό φίδι μιά ἐκείνη· καί περιμένει. Ὁ κύκλος στόν ἀέρα ἰσοῦται μέ πολλές μικρές κινήσεις ὁριζόντιες στό χῶμα. Ὁ κύκλος τῆς ἐπίθεσης νά σπάζει καί νά κολλᾶ κατόπιν τά κομμάτια του ἀργά σέ τεθλασμένη τροχιά. Ἄν ὁ τροχός ἀγγίξει τό φίδι πρίν προλάβει νά συρθεῖ στούς θάμνους, τότε τοῦ κόβει τό κεφάλι καί νικᾶ, τότε νικᾶ βγάζοντας σπίθες σάν ὁ τροχός πού ἀκονίζει τά μαχαίρια. Τότε νικᾶ μέ τελευταία κίνηση γοργή· ἡ κίνηση γοργή τοῦ θάνατου καί ξαναβρίσκει ὁ κύκλος τή στιλπνή του περιφέρεια.

Ἄν πάλι τό φίδι προλάβει καί κρυφτεῖ στούς θάμνους, γρήγορα βγάζει τό πουκάμισό του καί λάμπει σά σπαθί· εἶναι σπαθί. Τά πλαϊνά στηρίγματα, ἐκεῖ ὅπου τελειώνει ἡ λαβή κι ἀρχίζει τό λεπίδι, ἔγιναν φτερά. Πετᾶ καί κόβει τό λαιμό τῆς ἀετίνας. Ἐδῶ ἡ ὥρα τοῦ θανάτου γρήγορη, σφαίρα τοῦ αὐτόχειρα.

11. Slow game.

The wounded snake sets the pace of the game and the game could be called "the wounded snake." Not a sound, just as there is not a bitter bite in the cake: the snake's fresh wound should begin to bleed, a mute she-eagle out hunting, bushes that might save it.

The wounded snake sets the pace of the game. The she-eagle must not move too quickly; the agony of expressive movements; one contraction, the snake, the next, the she-eagle; and she waits. The circle in the air is equal to many small horizontal movements on the ground. The circle of attack should break apart and then slowly rearrange the pieces in a zigzag orbit. If the wheel touches the snake before it manages to drag itself into the bushes, then she cuts off its head and wins, then she wins letting off sparks like a wheel that sharpens knives. Then she wins with one last swift move; the swift move of death and the circle recovers its smooth circumference.

If, on the other hand, the snake manages to hide in the bushes, it quickly sheds its skin and shines like a sword; it is a sword. The hilt, where the handle ends and the blade begins, becomes wings. It takes off and cuts the she-eagle's throat. Here the hour of death is the swift bullet of the suicide.

12. Ρωμαϊκό μαρμάρινο ανάγλυφο, όπου ό αετός κρατά στά νύχια του τό φίδι καί πετά.

Ή αετίνα έχει τά βυζιά τής σφίγγας καί τή σιωπηλή της απειλή. Είναι γυναίκα μέ φτερά. Τό φίδι σιδερένιο σώμα άκαμπτο καί δυό εὐλύγιστα φτερά. Κι οἱ δυό μπορούνε νά σκοτώσουν καί νά σκοτωθοῦν.

Ή σφίγγα φοράει τό καλό της φόρεμα καί κουβαλᾶ πετώντας ένα κέικ γαρνιρισμένο μέ κεράσια. Τό φίδι φορᾶ τά ρούχα τοῦ κυνηγοῦ· κουρντίζει έρποντας τό ξυπνητήρι.

Ή αετίνα εἶναι κυνηγός. Τό φίδι κυνηγιέται.

12. A Roman marble relief, in which the he-eagle holds the snake in his talons and flies away.

The she-eagle has the sphinx's breasts and her silent threat. She is a woman with wings. The snake a metal inflexible body and two supple wings. Both can kill and be killed.

The sphinx wears her best dress and carries a cake decorated with cherries as she flies. The snake wears the hunter's clothes; and winds the alarm clock by crawling.

The she-eagle is the hunter. The snake is being hunted.

13. Τό πέταγμα τῆς ἀετίνας καί τοῦ φιδιοῦ τό πέταγμα πού εἶναι μίμηση· ἡ μίμηση τῆς φύσης γιά τό θάνατο τῆς φύσης εἶναι.

Τό πέταγμα τῆς ἀετίνας παράταση τοῦ παιχνιδιοῦ, κίνδυνος κάποιας ἥττας καί ἡδονή μιᾶς ἥττας θεατρικῆς.

Στό τέλος ἡ ἀετίνα θά πεῖ «καληνύχτα» στό φίδι καί θά γυρίσει στή φωλιά της. Τό φίδι θά πεῖ «καληνύχτα» στήν ἀετίνα καί θά γυρίσει στή δική του τρύπα. Κανένας δέ θυμᾶται ποιός σκότωσε σήμερα ποιόν.

13. The flight of the she-eagle and the flight of the snake which is imitation; the imitation of nature is for the death of nature.

The flight of the she-eagle, an extension of the game, the danger of some defeat and the pleasure of a theatrical defeat.

In the end the she-eagle will say "goodnight" to the snake and return to her nest. The snake will say "goodnight" to the she-eagle and return to his hole. No one remembers who killed who today.

Δ΄
Στό κρεβάτι

IV

In Bed

14. Ἐσύ θά πεῖς «καληνύχτα» στόν κυνηγό κι ὁ κυνηγός θά σοῦ πεῖ «καληνύχτα». Τότε ὁ νικημένος θά γυρίσει νά κοιμηθεῖ. Ὁ νικημένος σβήνει· σβήνει τό φῶς στό κομοδίνο γιά νά κοιμηθεῖ. Ὁ νικητής θά διαβάσει ἀκόμη λίγο προσέχοντας· τότε ὁ νικητής δέν κάνει φασαρία μήπως ξυπνήσει τόν ἄλλο. Ὁ νικητής θά σβήσει σέ λίγο τό φῶς ἀπ' τό δικό του κομοδίνο γιά νά κοιμηθεῖ. Ὁ νικητής κοιμᾶται. Ὁ νικημένος ξαγρυπνᾶ· τραβηγμένος στήν ἄκρη τοῦ διπλοῦ κρεβατιοῦ ξαγρυπνᾶ· στήν ἄκρη τῆς θάλασσας ξαγρυπνᾶ· ἐκεῖ στό θερινό καφενεῖο· ἐκεῖ πίνοντας οὖζο ξαγρυπνᾶ κι ἡ θάλασσα. Ἡ θάλασσα μεγάλο γκρίζο ταψί· ρευστή ἰσορροπία τοῦ γκρίζου καί τοῦ σκούρου μπλέ ἡ θάλασσα. Ἡ κόκκινη κουκκίδα ἀκίνητη μικρή· κουκκίδα μπάλα τοῦ πίνγκ-πόνγκ, ἀλλά μπορεῖ νά εἶναι καί τό κομμάτι κέικ πού βαφτίστηκε στό αἷμα· μπορεῖ. Κανένας, μονάχα ἕνας κύριος ἐπί τῶν ὑδάτων μέ μιά στόν ὦμο του πετσέτα διασχίζει τό μεγάλο γκρίζο ταψί καί φέρνει σ' ἕνα πιατάκι τήν κόκκινη κουκκίδα καρφωμένη σέ μιάν ὀδοντογλυφίδα γιά μεζέ. Βαδίζοντας λικνιστικά ἡ στρουθοκάμηλος σ' ἐκείνη τήν ταινία διέσχισε τήν μισοφωτισμένη ἔρημο μιᾶς κρεβατοκάμαρας. Κανένας δέ θυμᾶται ποιός σκότωσε σήμερα ποιόν ὅταν τελειώσει τό παιχνίδι. Ἡ μνήμη ἀμείλικτη ἀρετή τῶν δωματίων καί τῶν ἐπίπλων, ὅπου τά σώματα. Μνήμη τῶν ὅσων κυοφόρησαν τόν ὀργασμό δύο σωμάτων στό διάλειμμα τοῦ παιχνιδιοῦ.

14. You will say "goodnight" to the hunter and the hunter will say "goodnight" to you. Then the vanquished will roll over and go to sleep. The vanquished turns off; turns off the light on the bedside table in order to go to sleep. The victor will read a little longer taking care; now the victor keeps quiet not wanting to wake the other. In a while the victor will turn off the light on his bedside table and go to sleep. The victor sleeps. The vanquished stays awake; hugging the edge of the double bed he stays awake; at the edge of the sea he stays awake; there at the outdoor café; there drinking ouzo he stays awake and the sea. The sea is a big grey baking pan; the sea, a fluid balance of grey and dark blue. The red dot, small, immobile; the dot of a ping-pong ball, or perhaps the piece of cake that was baptized in blood, perhaps. No one, except a man walking on water with a napkin over his shoulder; he traverses the big grey baking pan and carries the red dot at the end of a toothpick on a plate as an hors d'oeuvre. Walking with a swaying motion, the ostrich in that film traversed the dimly lit desert of a bedroom. No one remembers today when the game is over who killed who. Memory, the implacable virtue of rooms and furniture, where the bodies. Memory of those pregnant with the orgasm of two bodies during the game's intermission.

15. Τῶν ὅσων κυοφόρησαν τόν ὕπνο.

Ἡ ἀετίνα ἀνοίγει τήν ντουλάπα καί βγάζει ἕνα κρεμαστάρι ἀπό σύρμα τυλιγμένο σέ πράσινο νάϋλον. Ντουλάπα μέ τά τρία φύλλα καί τά τέσσερα συρτάρια, ἐντοιχισμένη καί ἡ ἀετίνα τήν ἀνοίγει ὅλη γιά νά βγάλει ἕνα κρεμαστάρι πράσινο. Βγάζει τό κρεμαστάρι μέ τά ροῦχα τοῦ κυνηγοῦ, γιατί ὁ κυνηγός κρεμᾶ τά ροῦχα του ἀνάποδα στό πράσινο τσιγκέλι. Ἡ ἀετίνα ξεκουμπώνει τ' ἄδεια ροῦχα· τά δάχτυλα μέσα στά ροῦχα πού δέν ἔχουν σπλάχνα οὔτε σκοῦρο παγωμένο αἷμα, ἔντερα συκώτι καί καρδιά κι ἀνύπαρκτο σημεῖο σήψης καί τή ζέστα τῆς ζωῆς στήν τελευταία ἑτοιμόρροπη σταγόνα, τά δάχτυλα μέσα σέ ἄδεια ροῦχα καί τραβᾶ τά χέρια της γιατί ξεκούμπωσε ὅλα τά κουμπιά καί ξεκρεμᾶ τά ροῦχα γιά νά τά φορέσει. Ἡ ἀετίνα φορᾶ τά ροῦχα τοῦ κυνηγοῦ, φορᾶ μαῦρο κουστούμι καί γραβάτα, μαύρη ρεπούμπλικα κι ἄσπρο πουκάμισο, φορᾶ τό βλέμμα κατευθείαν μπροστά, φορᾶ τό ξυπνητήρι σέ μιά τσέπη κρεμασμένο μέ ἀλυσιδίτσα, τό βγάζει γιά νά τό κουρντίσει κι ἐξακριβώνει τό τίκ-τάκ στό δεξιό αὐτί λυγίζοντας τό κατευθείαν μπροστά βλέμμα· εἶναι ἡ ὥρα γιά νά βγεῖ καί νά σέ κυνηγήσει καί τραβᾶ τό ἔνδοξο σπαθί ἀπό τή θήκη καί σταματᾶ τόν ἦχο τῶν σιντριβανιῶν πού σιγοσφύριζε καί καμαρώνεται πρίν βγεῖ σ' ἕνα καθρέφτη τοῦ ξενοδοχείου. Ἑνός ξενοδοχείου μέ ἀπέραντους διαδρόμους. Κρύβεται μέσα στούς διαδρόμους τοῦ λαβύρινθου· ἔτσι κρυφή κι ἐλέγχοντας τά μυστικά του μέ τόν μίτο τοῦ ὀμφάλιου λώρου· ἔτσι σά φί-

15. About those who were pregnant with sleep.

The she-eagle opens the wardrobe and takes out a wire hanger wrapped in green plastic. A wardrobe with three doors and four drawers, built into the wall and the she-eagle opens it all just to get a green hanger. She takes the hanger with the hunter's clothes since the hunter hangs his clothes upside down on a green meat hook. The she-eagle unbuttons the empty clothes; the fingers inside the clothes which have no entrails, no dark congealed blood, intestines, liver, or heart, no absent signs of decay, nor the warmth of something living in the last pendulous drop, the fingers in the empty clothes and she withdraws her hands since she unbuttoned all the buttons and she takes the clothes off the hanger to wear them. The she-eagle wears the hunter's clothes, she wears a black suit and tie, black fedora and white shirt, she wears a look straight ahead, she wears an alarm clock in a pocket on a chain, she takes it out to wind it and checks the ticking by holding it to her right ear, tilting her straight-ahead look. It is time for her to go out and hunt you and she withdraws the glorious sword from its case and puts an end to the sound of fountains, that slow whistle, before she appears in the hotel mirror. A hotel with infinite corridors. She hides in the labyrinthine corridors; this way hidden and checking his secrets with the thread of the umbilical

δι κουλουριασμένο στήν κρυφή φωλιά του γεννᾶ τ' αὐγά κι ἔχει τό θηλυκό του κύκλο κάθε πού ἀλλάζει τό πουκάμισό του. Τό φίδι 'Αριάδνη.

cord; this way like a snake curled up in its secret den it lays eggs and has its feminine cycle every time it sheds its skin. The Ariadne snake.

16. Στήν τζαμαρία τῆς ἐξόδου κρέμεται ἕνα μικρό χαρτόνι μέ τά λόγια:

«Μήν ἀνησυχεῖτε. Ἀφῆστε τό πτῶμα μέσα στό ξενοδοχεῖο. Τό ἀναλαμβάνουμε ἐμεῖς. Τό φύλο του, ὅπως καί τό δικό σας, δέν μᾶς ἐνδιαφέρει. Εὐχαριστοῦμε γιά τήν προσπάθεια πού καταβάλατε ὥστε νά ἐπικρατήσει ἡ σωστή γραμμή».

16. Hanging on the glass exit door is a small piece of cardboard with the words:

"Don't worry. Leave the corpse in the hotel. We take full responsibility for it. Like yours, its sex is of no interest to us. Thank you for your assistance in ensuring the correct policy was implemented."

17. Οἱ πρῶτες ἄσπρες τρίχες ἑνός μήλου, ὅταν τό μῆλο σκίζεται σέ δυό κομμάτια. Τό ἕνα κομμάτι πρόσωπο τοῦ νικητῆ. Τό ἄλλο, ἐπίσης πρόσωπο τοῦ νικητῆ. Τό πρόσωπο πάνω στό τζάμι. Ἡ τζαμαρία τῆς ἐξόδου πάντοτε καθρέφτης. Μετέωρα μάτια διαβάζουν τά λόγια τῆς ἐπιγραφῆς· μετέωρο στόμα συλλαβίζει τά λόγια τῆς ἐπιγραφῆς. Τό ἕνα μάτι κρύβεται μές' στά μαλλιά: κάτι δέν εἶναι ἡ γλώσσα του, ἤ αὐτό πού ἀκούει, ἤ ἐκεῖνο πού διαβάζει· ἀλλά καί τά δυό μαζί δέν εἶναι ἡ γλώσσα του, μιά γλώσσα μητρική. Τό ἄλλο μάτι χτυπᾶ τόν χαρτονένιο στόχο πάνω στήν τζαμόπορτα, τόν διακορεύει, μπαίνει στόν κόλπο τῆς Ἀθήνας καί σταματᾶ σέ μιά ταράτσα. Κάτω οἱ πολυκατοικίες ν' ἀχνίζουν τή θυσία τῆς νικημένης πόλης στόν καταχτητή. Τό μάτι νά τυλίγεται ἀνασαίνοντας βαθιά γιά νά ξεκουραστεῖ στό σύννεφο τῆς ζέστης καί τοῦ καυσαέριου. Δέν ἐνοχλεῖται οὔτε ἀπό τό μόνο θόρυβο, τή φασαρία πού κάνουν οἱ μαστόροι προσπαθώντας ν' ἀλλάξουν τό σπασμένο τζάμι, νά περάσουν ἕνα καινούριο καί νά κρεμάσουν ἕνα χαρτονάκι μέ κάτι ξένα γράμματα, τά ἴδια πού μάταια προσπάθησαν καί χθές μέ καλαμπούρια νά διαβάσουν.

Τό πρῶτο μάτι εἶναι βουβό καί θηλυκό καί στεῖρο, ὅμως, ἄν γεννήσει, τό παιδί του θά 'χει τή δόξα τῆς μητροκτονίας. Τό πρῶτο μάτι φοβᾶται μέσα σέ μαλλιά πού ἀσπρίζουν κι ἀθέατο ἀκολουθεῖ τό ἄλλο μάτι. Ὁ νικητής δείχνει μόνο τό δεύτερο μάτι του.

17. The first white fibers of an apple when the apple is cut in two. The one piece, the face of the victor. The other, also the face of the victor. The face in the windowpane. The glass exit door is always a mirror. The eyes in midair read the words on the notice; the mouth in midair pronounces the words on the notice. One eye hidden in hair: something is not its language, either what it is hearing, or what it is reading; even the two together are not its language, a mother tongue. The other eye hits the cardboard target on the glass door, it ravishes it, enters Athens' bay and stops at a terrace. Below, the apartment buildings are steaming from the sacrifice of the vanquished city to the conqueror. The eye wraps itself up, breathing deeply in order to rest in the clouds of heat and exhaust. It is not bothered by the only sound, the racket that the builders make as they try to change the broken windowpane, to put in a new one and to hang a bit of cardboard with some foreign writing on it, the same one they tried in vain to read yesterday with much joking.

The first eye is mute and feminine and barren, however, if it gives birth, its child shall have the glory of matricide. The first eye is scared, hidden in hair which is turning white, unseen it follows the other eye. The victor only shows his second eye.

18. Παράτησες τό κέικ στό κομοδίνο καί τρέχεις νά δεῖς· εἶναι ἕνα μάτι σάν ποντίκι καθισμένο στό τσιμέντο τῆς ταράτσας. Κάπου-κάπου σαλεύει τ' ὀπτικό του νεῦρο σάν οὐρά. Παράτησες τό κέικ καί χαζεύεις τό μάτι πού εἶναι σάν ποντίκι, γυμνό καί κοιτᾶς ἐκεῖ νά δεῖς τό φύλο του. Δέν ἔχει φύλο. Εἶναι γυμνό καί σύ κοιτᾶς τήν ἴριδα. Πίσω ἀπό τό φακό της δουλεύει ἕνα ξυπνητήρι. Κόκκινο ξυπνητήρι. Ὅπως οἱ φλέβες πού σφίγγουν τόν βολβό. Κόκκινο δίχτυ. Ἐσύ τό 'ριξες· ἔπιασες ἕνα σπερματοζωάριο καί θά γεννήσεις. Δέν θέλεις ὅμως νά γεννήσεις αὐτό τό παιδί. Δέν θέλεις νά 'χεις αἰδοῖο καί γι' αὐτό. Γι' αὐτό ἁρπάζεις τό ποντίκι ἀπό τήν οὐρά καί τό πετᾶς στό δρόμο. Νά τό πατήσει μιά μοτοσιχλέτα.

18. You left the cake on the bedside table and you run to see; an eye like a mouse is sitting on the terrace pavement. Every once in a while it wags its optical nerve like a tail. You left the cake and you stare at the eye which is like a mouse, all naked and you look to check its sex. It has no sex. It is naked and you look at its iris. Behind its lens an alarm clock is ticking. A red alarm clock. Like the veins which squeeze the eyeball. A red net. You abort it; you caught a spermatozoon and you will give birth. But you do not want to give birth to that child. And you do not want to have a vagina and that's why. That's why you snatch the mouse by its tail and throw it in the road. So a motorcycle will run it over.

19. Κάθεσαι στό κρεβάτι. Ὁ κυνηγός εἶναι ἔξω στό μπαλκόνι, κάθεται σέ μιά πολυθρόνα πάνινη μασώντας ἕνα κομμάτι ἀπό τό κέικ πού βρέθηκε στό κομοδίνο. Ἄν εἶσαι τό βουβό νερό γεμάτου ποτηριοῦ ἐκεῖνος εἶναι τό βουβό ποτήρι τοῦ νεροῦ, ἤ τό ἀντίθετο. Ἄν εἶσαι ὁ κώδικας τοῦ ἐρωτικοῦ μαρκήσιου στή φυλακή, ὁ κυνηγός μιλᾶ τή γλώσσα τοῦ πατριαρχικοῦ ἀφορισμοῦ τῆς ἐπανάστασης, ἤ τό ἀντίθετο. Ἄν εἶσαι ἡ ματωμένη ἀπεργία τοῦ Σικάγου, αὐτός στό Μεξικό δολοφονεῖ τόν Τρότσκυ, ἤ τό ἀντίθετο. Ἄν εἶσαι ἰσορροπιστής, ὁ κυνηγός δέν ἔχει ἄλλο τρόπο γιά νά ζεῖ κοντά σου κι ὁρίζει τήν πόζα στερεότυπης φωτογραφίας καί μέ τό δεξί πατᾶ ἕνα μεγάλο σῶμα, τό δικό σου, σωριασμένο παράλληλα στ' ὄρθιο σῶμα τῆς μοτοσικλέτας, ἤ τό ἀντίθετο. Ζυγίζεις πόσος ὁρισμός καί πόσο σῶμα: οἱ ὁρισμοί δέν ἀνταλλάσσονται, ὅπως δέν ἀνταλλάσσονται τά σώματα ποτέ. Τά σώματα δανείζουν κάποτε τίς φορεσιές. Τό ροῦχο τοῦ ὁρισμοῦ εἶναι ἡ ἴδια ἡ διατύπωσή του καί κουρελιάζεται μαζί της. Τά σώματα μένουν γυμνά καί ὄρθια καί πέφτοντας τρυποῦν τήν ἀτσαλένια ἐπιφάνεια τοῦ νεροῦ. Ἕνα ταψί γεμάτο τρύπες ξαφνικές ἐφήμερες, ἕνα ταψί τῶν ἐπετείων γεμάτο τρύπες τῶν σωμάτων. Καί ξαναζυγίζεις πόσοι ὁρισμοί καί πόσα σώματα.

19. You sit on the bed. The hunter is outside on the balcony, he sits in a deck chair chewing on a piece of the cake that was on the bedside table. If you are the mute water of the full glass, he is the mute glass of water, or the other way around. If you are the code of the erotic marquis in jail, the hunter speaks the patriarch's language of excommunicating revolutionaries, or the other way around. If you are the bloody strike in Chicago, he is in Mexico murdering Trotsky, or the other way around. If you are the one in a balancing act, the hunter has no other means of living near you and he sets up a stereotypical photograph pose with his right foot on a big body, your body, in a heap parallel to the upright body of the motorcycle, or the other way around. You weigh the amount of definition and the amount of body: the definitions never replace each other, just as the bodies never replace each other. Sometimes the bodies lend their costumes. The definition's clothing is the same as its wording and both are torn to shreds. The bodies remain naked and upright and falling make holes in the water's steel surface. A baking pan full of sudden, ephemeral holes, an anniversary baking pan full of bodies' holes. And again you weigh the amount of definitions and the amount of bodies.

Ε´

Ὁ θάνατος καί ἡ κηδεία

V

The Death and the Funeral

20. Θά 'ναι λοιπόν αὐτοκτονία ἤ δολοφονία; Ποτέ στό φῶς τῆς μέρας, ἀκόμη καί χειμωνιάτικης. Οὔτε τίς ὧρες ὅποιου δειλινοῦ. Ἕνας γλόμπος ἑκατό κηρίων στό ταβάνι. Ἑκατό κεριά σ' ἕνα κρεμαστό κέικ γενεθλίων, στό ταβάνι τοῦ σαλονιοῦ μέ τά γύψινα ἀγγελούδια. Πάνω στόν ρόζ βελουδένιο καναπέ εἶναι ξαπλωμένο τό γυναικεῖο σῶμα. Ἡ αὐτοκτονία μόλις ἔχει γίνει. Φορᾶ τό δέρμα της χλωμό. Τό φῶς τοῦ γλόμπου ἑστιάζεται στά χέρια της. Τό ἕνα χέρι τῆς πεθαμένης εἶναι τό χέρι τοῦ κυνηγοῦ. Τό δεξί. Τό ὑπόλοιπο σῶμα τῆς ἀνήκει. Ἤ, πάνω στόν ρόζ βελουδένιο καναπέ εἶναι ξαπλωμένο τό γυναικεῖο σῶμα. Ἡ δολοφονία μόλις ἔχει γίνει. Πίσω ἀπό κάθε ἔπιπλο καί πίσω ἀπό κάθε πόρτα κρύβεται ὁ μοναδικός δολοφόνος. Φορᾶ μαῦρο κουστούμι καί γραβάτα, μαύρη ρεπούμπλικα κι ἄσπρο πουκάμισο. Κοιτάζει κατευθείαν μπροστά. Ὄρθιος. Τό φῶς τοῦ γλόμπου ἑστιάζεται στά χέρια του. Τό ἕνα χέρι τοῦ δολοφόνου εἶναι τό χέρι τῆς πεθαμένης. Τό δεξί. Τό ὑπόλοιπο σῶμα τοῦ ἀνήκει.

Τό χέρι τῆς γυναίκας πού εἶναι γυναικεῖο, τό χέρι τοῦ ἄντρα πού εἶναι ἀντρικό, ἁπλώνεται καί κλείνει τόν διακόπτη. Σβήνει τά κεράκια τοῦ κέικ. Θά τό κόψει καί θά τό μοιράσει σ' ὅσους ἔρθουν.

20. So, will it be suicide or murder? Never in the light of day, even of a winter day. Not even in the hours of any dusk. A bulb the power of a hundred candles on the ceiling. A hundred candles on a hanging birthday cake on the ceiling with the plaster cherubs. The woman's body is laid out on the red velvet settee. The suicide has just taken place. She is wearing her skin pale. The light from the bulb focuses on her hands. One of the dead woman's hands is the hunter's. The right one. The rest of her body belongs to her. Or, the woman's body is laid out on the red velvet setee. The murder has just taken place. Behind every piece of furniture and every door the sole murderer is hiding. He wears a black suit and tie, black fedora and white shirt. He looks straight ahead. Standing there. The light from the bulb focuses on his hands. One of the murderer's hands is the dead woman's. The right one. The rest of his body belongs to him.

The hand of the woman which is feminine, the hand of the man which is masculine, stretches out and turn off the switch. It extinguishes the candles on the cake. It will cut it and divide it among those who come.

21. Ἡ πομπή τους, στοιχισμένοι ἄντρας γυναίκα, ὅλοι φίλοι καί κρατοῦν ἕνα κλωνάρι ἀνθισμένης κερασιᾶς. Ἀνοίγουν τήν πόρτα τοῦ μπαλκονιοῦ. Ἔχει ξημερώσει. Κοιτάζουν πρῶτα τό σαλόνι, τούς σοβάδες πού κρέμονται ἀπό τό ταβάνι, τήν ὑγρασία στόν τοῖχο μέ τό καλοριφέρ, τούς λεκέδες στό πάτωμα. Μετά κοιτάζουν τό μόνο πράγμα στό δωμάτιο: τό νεκρό σῶμα πάνω στό παρκέ. Μέ μικρά βήματα σχηματίζουν βουβοί ἕνα κύκλο γύρω του, ἔνοχα βήματα κι ἐκεῖνοι θαυμάζοντας. Ἄντρας γυναίκα μέ σειρά χοροῦ ἀφήνουν τρυφερά πάνω του τά κλωνάρια τους. Ὅταν κι ἡ τελευταία χειρονομία ἔχει γίνει, κάθονται κάτω. Κάθονται καί περιμένουν.

Οἱ γυναῖκες φοροῦν τό δέρμα τους χλωμό. Τό δεξί τους χέρι εἶναι τοῦ κυνηγοῦ.

Οἱ ἄντρες φοροῦν μαῦρο κουστούμι καί γραβάτα, μαύρη ρεπούμπλικα κι ἄσπρο πουκάμισο. Κοιτάζουν κατευθείαν μπροστά. Τό δεξί τους χέρι εἶναι τῆς πεθαμένης.

Περιμένουν καί βλέπουν. Ἡ γύρη χτίζει πάνω στό λείψανο κουβούκλιο τοῦ μαρτυρίου. Ὕπεροι ἀνοίγουν τά χείλια καί κοινωνοῦν τόν ἔρωτα τῆς γύρης. Τό κεφάλι τῶν λουλουδιῶν φουσκώνει, τά πέταλα ζαρώνουν καί πέφτουν. Ὁ καρπός σκληρός καί λαμπρός, τά καινούρια κεράσια.

Τρῶνε τώρα τό κέικ γαρνιρισμένο μέ πολύ κερασάκι γλυκό. Κανένας δέν σηκώνεται γιά νά φιλήσει.

21. Their procession is arranged a man, then a woman, they are all friends and they hold a branch of cherry blossoms. They open the balcony door. Morning has broken. They look first at the living room, at the bits of plaster hanging from the ceiling, the dampness on the wall with the radiator, the stains on the floor. Next they look at the only thing in the room: the dead body on the parquet. Silently and with small steps they form a circle around it, guilty steps and they are in awe. A man, then a woman like in a dance they place their branches gently on top of it. And when the last gesture is finished they sit down. They sit and wait.

The women wear their skin pale. Their right hand is the hunter's.

The men wear black suits and ties, black fedoras and white shirts. They look straight ahead. Their right hand is the dead woman's.

They wait and see. The pollen builds a martyr's tomb over the mortal remains. The pistils open their lips and receive the pollen's love. The flower center swells, the petals dry up and fall off. The new cherries are its hard, shiny fruit.

They eat the cake which is now decorated with lots of cherries in syrup. No one gets up to kiss. It has been awhile since the dead woman went to the neighboring

Ἡ πεθαμένη ἔχει ὥρα πού ἔφυγε καί πάει στό διπλανό οἰκόπεδο νά κρεμαστεῖ στήν ἀνθισμένη κερασιά. Ἀφοῦ δοκίμασε ἄν ἔδεσε τό σιρόπι καί τό βρῆκε ἐντάξει.

lot to hang herself in the cherry tree. After she tested
the syrup to see if it had set and found it adequate.

22. Ἀλλά δέν κρεμιέται. Περιμένει. Ἡ πομπή τους καταφτάνει, στοιχισμένοι ἄντρας γυναίκα καί κρατοῦν τό μισοφαγωμένο κομμάτι κέικ μέ τό κερασάκι. Τό στόμα τους εἶναι πασαλειμμένο μέ τό κόκκινο σιρόπι. Στό οἰκόπεδο δέν βλέπουν καμιά κερασιά, μά θά μποροῦσαν σ' ἕνα σίδερο ἀπό τή στέγη τῆς παράγκας ἄν στηριχτοῦνε ὄρθιοι στή σέλα τῆς μοτοσικλέτας, ἤ θά μποροῦσανε σέ κάτι ἐξίσου στέρεο κι εὐθύ — σ' ἕνα εὐτυχισμένο βλέμμα ἀγάπης θά μποροῦσαν.

Ἀλλά δέν κρεμιέται γιατί στό οἰκόπεδο τοῦ πάρκινγκ δέν ὑπάρχει παράγκα. Τότε ἡ πεθαμένη φοβᾶται καί συντάσσεται μέ τήν πομπή τους. Στοιχισμένοι ἄντρας γυναίκα καί κρατοῦν τήν τελευταία αἰσιόδοξη διέξοδο σ' ἕνα μικρό πακέτο. Ἡ πομπή ὅλοι ντυμένοι τά καθημερνά τους ροῦχα κι ἀρχίζει νά διαλύεται, μά δέν βαδίζουν πιά τό ἴδιο. Ἡ πομπή χωρίζεται στά δυό, ἀλλοῦ οἱ ἄντρες ἀλλοῦ οἱ γυναῖκες. Δύο σειρές ἀνθρώπινες φιγοῦρες, κομμένες μέ ψαλίδι σέ λεπτό χαρτόνι καί κρατημένες χέρι-χέρι καθώς φεύγουν. Οἱ ἄντρες κολλοῦν τά χαρτονένια σώματά τους συμμετρικά καί γίνονται ἕνας. Οἱ γυναῖκες κολλοῦν τά χαρτονένια σώματά τους συμμετρικά καί γίνονται ἐσύ. Ἐσύ νά τρέχεις στό ταψί τοῦ ἄδειου πάρκινγκ χαρτονένια καί τό δεξί σου χέρι μέ τό κέικ χέρι τοῦ κυνηγοῦ. Πίσω σου τρέχει ὁ χαρτονένιος ἕνας, μέ τό δεξί του χέρι τό δικό σου νά κουρντίζει τό ξυπνητήρι.

Ὅλα τά σώματα κομμένα ἴδια κι οἱ κινήσεις ἀπαράλλαχτες.

22. But she doesn't hang herself. She waits. The procession arrives unexpectedly, arranged a man, then a woman and they are holding the half-eaten piece of cake with the tiny cherry. Their mouths are smeared with red syrup. They cannot see a single cherry tree in the lot, but they could, from one of the hut's steel roof beams if they stood on the saddle of the motorcycle, or they could from something similarly solid and straight —from a blissful look of love they could.

But she does not hang herself because there is no hut in the lot. Then the dead woman gets scared and joins their procession. Arranged a man, then a woman and they hold the last optomistic way out in a small packet. All dressed in their everyday clothes, the procession begins to dissolve, since they are no longer walking in step. The procession breaks into two, over there the men, over there the women. Two lines of human figures, cut out of cardboard with scissors, holding hands as they peel off. The men glue their cardboard bodies together symmetrically and become you. The women glue their cardboard bodies together symmetrically and become you. Cardboard, you should run to the baking pan of the empty parking lot and your right hand with the cake is the hunter's. Behind you runs the one cardboard man, with his right hand your hand winding the alarm clock.

All the bodies are cut the same and their movements are identical.

ΣΤ′

Τώρα ἐγώ

VI

Now Me

23. Τὸ σῶμα μου ὅλα τά χαρτονένια σώματα τῶν γυναικῶν καί φτάνω στήν ἄκρη τοῦ ἄδειου πάρκινγκ. Καί φτάνω στήν ἄκρη τοῦ ἄδειου ταψιοῦ. Φορῶ τήν ὀργαντίνα μέ τά τρία βολάν πού καταλήγουνε σέ δαντελίτσα, ἄσπρα καλτσάκια καί παπούτσια. Φορῶ βρεγμένα τά μαλλιά μου κατσαρά μέ τή χωρίστρα στό ἕνα πλάι καί στό ἄλλο τό κοκαλάκι νά στηρίζει τήν μεγάλη μπούκλα. Φορῶ στή μιά μου φούχτα δυό λουλούδια γιά νά τά πετάξω στήν πλατεία καί κουβαλῶ στό ἄλλο χέρι τό κέικ μέ τά κερασάκια. Τό ἀκουμπῶ ἐπάνω στή σκηνή κοντά στά δυό μου πόδια πού γωνιάζουν μέ τίς φτέρνες ἑνωμένες. Καί ὑποκλίνομαι γιά τούς μεγάλους καί γιά τή σκόνη πού περιμένει στίς κουρτίνες. Τό πρόσωπό μου ἀπό κάτω πρός τά πάνω λοξά εἶναι τό κέλυφος τοῦ νοικοκυρεμένου ἴαμβου. Φωνή σφυρί τό σπᾶ μέ κίνηση λοξή πάνω πρός κάτω. Κρέμονται μέ σπαγκάκι τέσσερα κομμάτια στά κλαδιά τοῦ ψεύτικου ἔλατου καί περιμένουν σάν τό μῆλο τῆς Σαπφῶς ἀλλά χωρίς νά κοκκινίζουν. Τέσσερεις μύθοι κρεμασμένοι.

Ὁ πρῶτος μύθος μέ τό φεγγάρι.

Παλάμη μαλακιά σφουγγίζει τούς γοφούς τῆς ἱδρωμένης γυάλινης κανάτας. Μέσα της ἕνα ψάρι, κόκκινος πράσινος ἰχθύς κατακομβῶν, νά προφητεύει κολυμπώντας τίς καμπύλες. Βάζω τό δάκτυλό μου στό νερό. Τό ψάρι κάνει κύκλους. Ἀγγίζει μιά στιγμή τό δάκτυλό μου. Μεταμορφώνομαι σ' ἕνα τσαμπί μέ κόκκινους στρογγυλεμένους ὄγκους. Κάθε δυό ρῶγες

23. My body is all the cardboard bodies of women and I arrive at the edge of the empty parking lot. And I arrive at the edge of the empty baking pan. I wear organdy with three flounces that are trimmed in lace, white socks and shoes. I wear my hair wet and curly with the part on one side and on the other a barrette to keep the big curl in place. I wear two flowers in one of my palms so that I can throw them in the square and I carry the cake with the tiny cherries in the other. I rest it on the stage near my two feet which make a right angle where my heels join. And I bow for the grown ups and for the dust waiting in the curtains. My face at a slant from the bottom up is the shell of an orderly iamb. A voice like a hammer breaks it with an oblique motion from the top down. Four pieces are hanging by string from the branches of a fake fir tree and wait like Sappho's apple but they never grow red. Four myths are hanging.

The first myth with the moon.

A soft palm brushes the hips of the wet glass jug. Inside a fish, a red green ichthys from the catacombs prophesying the curves as it swims. I put my finger in the water. The fish makes circles. For one second it touches my finger. I turn into a stem of round, red grapes. Every two grapes, a deep vagina fissure in a sacred cave, in a three-room apartment. Ritual ablutions in a bathtub. My two bare hands are two trees of

μιά βαθιά ρωγμή αἰδοίου σέ σπήλαια ἱερά, σ' ἕνα τριάρι. Ἱερουργίες τοῦ ἀπολουσμοῦ σέ μιά μπανιέρα. Τά δυό γυμνά μου χέρια εἶναι δυό δέντρα γνώσης. Τά δυό δέντρα ριζώνουν στά δυό γυμνά βυζιά. Στά χέρια μου τυλίγονται δυό φίδια: ὁ γιός μου κι ὁ ἐραστής μου. Στό φῶς τοῦ φεγγαριοῦ.

Ὁ δεύτερος μύθος μέ τή λαμπάδα.

Τό μινωικό μου στῆθος θά μπορούσε νά 'ναι ἐκείνης τῆς Ἐλευθερίας ὁδηγώντας τό λαό. Τά φίδια γύρω στά γυμνά μου χέρια θά μπορούσαν νά 'χαν γίνει τουφέκι καί λάβαρο. Οἱ ὁριζόντιοι ἄντρες νεκροί, κάθετοι οἱ ζωντανοί. Ἐγώ, ἀνοίγοντας τά χέρια μέ τήν ὁρμή τοῦ βήματός μου, θά ἔγραφα τήν ὑποτείνουσα τοῦ νοητοῦ ὀρθογώνιου τριγώνου. Διαγωνίως θ' ἄγγιζα νεκρούς καί ζωντανούς καί θά προχώραγα.

Ἴσως θά μπορούσα νά μετατρέψω τήν ἡδονή τοῦ ἔρωτα στήν ἡδονή μιᾶς λαϊκῆς ἐξέγερσης. Ἴσως θά μπορούσα νά 'χα γεφυρώσει ζωή καί θάνατο σ' ἕνα ἁπλό γραμμικό σχῆμα πού σημαίνει ἐπίσης γέννηση. Ἴσως θά μπορούσα νά ἔσταζα ἀπ' τή λαμπάδα τοῦ ρομαντισμοῦ τό φῶς στό χέρι καί στό πόδι.

Τί κράτησα ἀπό τόν περασμένο αἰώνα;

Ὁ τρίτος μύθος μέ τόν ἠλεκτρισμό.

Τά ἠλεκτρικά λαμπιόνια τοῦ εἰκοστοῦ ἀναβοσβήνουν καί μέ δείχνουν ὅραμα τοῦ ἡγεμόνα καί τοῦ ἀρ-

knowledge. The two trees have their roots in two bare breasts. Two snakes wrap around my hands: my son and my lover. In the moonlight.

The second myth with the torch.

My minoan breast could be Liberty's as she leads the people. The snakes wrapped around my bare hands could have become rifle and banner. The horizontal men are corpses, the vertical ones are living. Opening my hands with the momentum of walking I would write the hypotenuse of a virtual triangle. Diagonally I would touch the dead and the living and proceed.

Perhaps I could have converted the pleasure of love into the pleasure of a popular uprising. Perhaps I could have bridged life and death in a simple line drawing that also means birth. Perhaps I could have draw from the torch of romanticism the light on the hand, the light on the foot.

What have I taken from the last century?

The third myth with electricity.

The electric lightbulbs of the twentieth century turn on and off and show me to be the vision of the sovereign and the architect, an invented woman, without a body, full of holes, the painting of the Big Tower of Babel. Red open doors give birth to sounds and white open doors mourn the chaos of tongues. Each

χιτέκτονα, γυναίκα ἐπινόημα, χωρίς κορμί γεμάτη τρύπες, ὁ πίνακας Μεγάλος Πύργος τῆς Βαβέλ. Κόκκινες ἀνοιχτές πόρτες γεννοῦνε ἤχους καί ἄσπρες ἀνοιχτές πενθοῦν τό χάος τῶν γλωσσῶν. Κάθε καμπύλη πλάι σ' ἄλλη μιά καμπύλη μέ ὁδηγεῖ στό στῆθος μου ἀνεστραμμένο. Ὁ πύργος εἶναι τό ἀντικείμενο τοῦ μηχανῶμαι κι ἐγώ μιά μηχανή. Ἡ μηχανή, τό τεράστιο θηλυκό, θρονιασμένη στή μέση τοῦ πίνακα, ξερή ἀλλά κυρίαρχη στ' ἀμυδρά λιβάδια, στά σπίτια, στή λίγη θάλασσα. Ἡ μηχανή, τό τεράστιο θηλυκό, ὑγρή, σκουριάζει τούς ἁρμούς πού συναρμολογοῦν μέ κόπο ὁ ἡγεμόνας καί ὁ ἀρχιτέκτονας στήν κάτω ἀριστερή ἄκρη τοῦ πίνακα. Ἄγλωσση τελευταία γέννα πολύφωνης καί ἀνεικονικῆς γυναίκας.

Ὁ τέταρτος μύθος μέ τόν καμένο γλόμπο.

Κάθε βράδυ ἀνάβω τόν καμένο γλόμπο τῆς ἠθικῆς μου νά γδυθῶ. Τό κρεμαστάρι ἀπό σύρμα τυλιγμένο μέ πράσινο νάυλον. Ἐκεῖ κρεμῶ τά ροῦχα, ὅταν ἀδειάζουν ἀπ' τό σῶμα μου. Ὅταν ἀνοίγω τά τρία φύλλα καί τά τέσσερα συρτάρια τῆς ἐντοιχισμένης ντουλάπας. Πῶς εἶναι τά φορέματα ὅταν γεμίζουν μέ τό σῶμα μου; Εἰσβάλλω σ' ὅλα τά ροῦχα καί σ' ὅλα τά ἐσώρουχα ταυτόχρονα. Πολλαπλασιάζομαι. Στριφογυρίζω πολλαπλή. Ψάχνω μέ τρυφερότητα νά βρῶ ἕνα λεκέ, ἕνα τσαλάκωμα, ἕνα ξήλωμα. Πηγαίνω μέχρι τό τραπέζι καί παίρνω ἕνα μαρκαδόρο χρωματιστό. Νά ζωγραφίσω κύκλους ὅπου θυμᾶμαι νά μέ ἄγγιξαν ἄλ-

curve next to another curve drives me back to my breast upside down. The tower is the object of contrivance and I am one machine. The machine, the huge feminine thing, enthroned in the middle of the painting, dry but dominating the faded pastures, the houses, the little bit of sea. The machine, the huge feminine thing, wet, rusts the joints which the sovereign and the architect assemble with difficulty in the lower left hand corner of the painting. The tongueless last born of the polyphonic and non-representational woman.

The fourth myth with the burned-out bulb.

Every evening I turn on the burned-out bulb of my ethics to undress. The wire hanger wrapped in green plastic. There I hang my clothes when they are emptied of my body. When I open the three doors and the four drawers of the wardrobe built into the wall. What are dresses like when they are full of my body? I invade all my clothes and underwear at the same time. I multiply. I whirl around multiplying. I hunt with tenderness for a stain, a crease, some undone stitching. I go up to the table and take a colored magic marker. To draw circles wherever I remember being touched by others. Small concentration camps from which I cannot escape and colored they begin to fade with smoke. Like colored smoke it will give the last kiss in a double bed; it will kiss the table and chairs and last of all the mirror. Paint brushes dipped in phosphorescent paints will color the

λοι ἄνθρωποι. Μικρά στρατόπεδα ἀπ' ὅπου δέν μπορῶ νά δραπεπτεύσω καί χρωματιστά θ' ἀρχίσουν νά ξεβάφουν μέ καπνούς. Ὡσάν χρωματιστοί καπνοί θά δώσουν τόν τελευταῖο ἀσπασμό σ' ἕνα διπλό κρεβάτι· τραπέζι καί καρέκλα θά φιλήσουν καί τόν καθρέφτη τελευταῖο. Πινέλα βουτηγμένα σέ φωσφορικές μπογιές θά βάφουν τόν ἀέρα μέ χρωματιστές λουρίδες κάθετες σέ μένα, ἔτσι ὅπως ἐγώ ἔχω ξαπλώσει στό κρεβάτι καί χαζεύω. Ἔτσι κοιτάζοντας τίς βδέλλες νά κολλᾶνε τή βεντούζα καί θ' ἀσελγήσουν γιά στερνή φορά, ἄσπρες σατέν λουρίδες ὑφασμάτων. Στήν ἀνοιχτή ντουλάπα τά σκισμένα ροῦχα θά μοιραστοῦνε ξαφνικά ὅπως τά βλέπω κι ἀνάμεσά τους ἕνα κατάμαυρο αἰδοῖο χωρίς ἴχνος κόκκινο. Καπνοί καί τούς χαζεύω καθώς φεύγουν διάφανοι ἀπ' τό μπαλκόνι.

air in stripes, vertical to me, now that I have laid myself out on the bed and I stare. In this position I watch the leeches stick on with suction cups and rape for the last time, white satin strips of material. In the open wardrobe the shredded clothes will separate suddenly before my eyes and among them a pitch-black vagina appears without a trace of red. I stare at the smoke as it leaves diaphanously from the balcony.

24. Τό σῶμα μου ὅλα τά χαρτονένια σώματα τῶν γυναικῶν καί φτάνω στήν ἄκρη ἑνός ἄδειου πάρκινγκ· καί φτάνω στήν ἄκρη τῶν μύθων. Φορῶ τό κερασί μου πέπλο κι ἀποπάνω τό δέρμα ἐλαφιοῦ. Φορῶ τούς βόστρυχους λυμένους καί τό στεφάνι μέ κισσό μέ φίδια καί μέ ἄσπρες φοῦντες. Φορῶ στή δεξιά μου φούχτα θύρσο καί στήν ἀριστερή τό φρυγικό μου τούμπανο. Καί ὑποκλίνομαι γιά τίς βελανιδιές καί τά ἐλάτια. Κινῶ τό ἄσπρο πόδι γιά τόν ὁλονύχτιο χορό καί κατεβαίνω ἀπό τή σκηνή στό δάσος. Μαζεύω τά ξερά κλαδιά γιά τή φωτιά. Χτυπῶ τό βράχο μέ τό θύρσο μου καί βγαίνει ζάχαρη. Ξύνω μέ τ' ἀκροδάχτυλα τή γῆ καί βγαίνει ἀλεύρι. Τό ρυάκι στάζει βούτυρο. Ὅλα τά χαρτονένια σώματα τῶν γυναικῶν στό σῶμα μου πού εἶναι ζυγαριά. Στή μιά παλάμη μου ἡ ζάχαρη, στήν ἄλλη ἀλεύρι. Τό σῶμα μου μέσ' στό καλό του φόρεμα ζυγίζει, μέσα στό κερασί του πέπλο καί τό δέρμα τοῦ ἐλαφιοῦ γιγαντιαῖο ἀκίνητο ζυγίζει μέ τήν εὐαίσθητη παλάμη πόσο ἀλεύρι, πόση ζάχαρη καί πόσο βούτυρο. Ρίχνω μετά μέσ' στό βουτυρωμένο τύμπανο τή ζύμη γιά νά φτιάξω κέικ φρυγικό μέ κερασάκια. Τό κέικ μέσ' στό φρυγικό ταψί κι ἐγώ μέσ' στήν κουζίνα μου βαδίζω κουβαλώντας ἕνα κεφάλι λιονταριοῦ στά χέρια. Ἕνα κεφάλι λιονταριοῦ μέσ' στήν κοιλιά μου. Αὐτό τ' ἀσώματο καί στρογγυλό κεφάλι πού θά δοκιμάσει τό γλυκό μου. Τό λιονταρίσιο του κεφάλι, πού θά ξεράσει τό γλυκό μου. Ἐγώ θά τό γεννῶ καί θά τό θανατώνω. Αὐτό τό λιονταρίσιο κεφάλι κυνηγοῦ. Καί θά σταλάξω δώδεκα κερασένιες ἐρωτήσεις γύρω-γύρω. Νά μοιάζει μέ ρο-

24. My body is all the cardboard bodies of women and I arrive at the edge of an empty parking lot; and I arrive at the edge of myths. I wear my cherry-colored veil and on top a deer hide. I wear loose curls and a crown of ivy, snakes and white tassels, a thyrsus in my right hand and a Phrygian drum in my left. And I bow to the fir trees and the oaks. I point my white foot for the night-long dance and I descend from the stage into the forest. I gather dry branches for a fire. I hit the stone with my thyrsus and sugar pours forth. I scratch the earth with my fingertips and flour pours forth. The stream drips butter. My body, a pair of scales, containing all the cardboard bodies of women. In one of my palms the sugar, in the other the flour. My body in its best dress weighs, in its cherry-colored veil and the deer hide gigantic, immobile it weighs with the sensitive palm the right amount of flour, of sugar, and of butter. Then I toss the dough into the buttered pan in order to make a Phrygian cake with tiny cherries. The cake is inside the Phrygian baking pan and I am inside my kitchen, I walk around carrying the lion head in my hands. A lion head in my belly. That round, bodiless head that will try my sweet. The lion head that will vomit my sweet. I will give birth to it and keep killing it. The hunter's lion head. And I will drop twelve cherry questions in a circle around the top. To look like a speedometer. The indicator on a motorboat and I will escape in that motorboat taking a violent turn and going the other way, after I bow to myself and bid farewell to the oaks and the firs,

λόι ταχυτήτων. Ὁ δείχτης μιᾶς βενζινακάτου κι ἐγώ στή βενζινάκατο θά δραπετεύσω τραβώντας βίαια τόν ἄλλο δρόμο, ἀφοῦ ὑποκλιθῶ καί χαιρετίσω βελανιδιές κι ἐλάτια τίς ξύλινες καρέκλες μέ τούς μεγάλους καί μέ τούς μικρότερους· ἀφήνοντας τή βάρκα δεμένη σ' ἕνα πάσσαλο τῆς λίμνης, τή λίμνη στό χαρτί ζωγραφισμένη καί τό χαρτί σελίδα γλώσσας πού ἔκλεισε σά λίμνη. Θ' ἀράξω σ' ἕνα τόπο ζεστό καί πράσινο μέ κίτρινη ἀμμουδιά καί φροῦτα στά δέντρα μέ τά ἐξωτικά πουλιά. Καί θά φυτέψω τά ροῦχα τῆς μαινάδας κοντά σέ μιά πηγή καί ἡ πηγή σ' ἕνα χαρτί ζωγραφισμένη καί τό χαρτί σελίδα γλώσσας πού ἀναβρύζει. Καί δίπλα θά ξαπλώσω ἤρεμη καί γυμνή γιά νά γεννήσω.

the wooden chairs with the grownups and the children; leaving the boat tied to a stake in the lake, the lake drawn on paper and the paper a page of language that closed like a lake. I will moor in a hot green country with yellow sands and fruit-laden trees and exotic birds. And I will plant the maenad's clothes near a spring and the spring drawn on paper and the paper a page of language that wells up. And next to this I will lie down, calm and naked, and give birth.

ΤΖΕΝΗ ΜΑΣΤΟΡΑΚΗ

Ἱστορίες
γιά τά βαθιά

ΔΕΥΤΕΡΗ ΕΚΔΟΣΗ

ΚΕΔΡΟΣ 1986

Τί σύμπτωσις, μοί εἶπε, κύριε!
Τί παράξενος σύμπτωσις σᾶς φέρει
εἰς τόν οἶκον τοῦ φονέως;

Tales of the Deep

by Jenny Mastoraki

"What coincidence, sir," he said to me,
"What strange coincidence brings you
  to the house of the murderer?"

Α΄
Συντομοτάτη περιγραφή τοῦ τόπου ἐκείνου ὅπου τελοῦνται ὅλα τά φοβερά

I
A Brief Description of the Place
Where Terrible Things Happened

Νά χυθεῖ πρῶτα πρῶτα βαρύς ὁ ἀέρας καί κόκκινος ἀπό χρόνιες μάχες.

Καί καπνοί ἀπό ὄρη ὅπου φέγγουν ἀρχαῖα χαλάσματα, παραστάσεις θριάμβων καί φόνων.

Σκιερός ὁ δρυμός γιά νά χάνονται βασιλεῖς νυχτοθῆρες, ἤ στασίαρχοι κάτωχροι ἀνασπώντας ἀγχέμαχα ὅπλα.

Ἀλλά μόνος παντοῦ ὁ κυνηγός καί ξοπίσω του διῶκτες.

Let the air first spill over, heavy and red after years of battle.

And the smoke from mountains where ancient ruins still glow, scenes of triumph and murder.

Let the forest be dark, so that kings on night-prowl lose their way, or the mutineers, pallid, unsheathing their daggers.

But the hunter alone everywhere with pursuers on his trail.

B′
Τά Πάθη τῆς Ἀγάπης

II
The Sufferings of Love

Τά ὑπόγεια

Σέ μυστικές στοές, μέ κρεμασμένους καί ὑδρό-
βια, καί μιά βουή σάν νά περνάει νερό. Πολύ
νερό.

Πίσω ἀπ' τούς τοίχους σέρνεται κάτι πελώριο
καί βαρύ, πού ἔχει βράσει σέ φριχτές φωτιές,
μπορεῖ πηγάδι, ἕνα ὑπόγειο πέρασμα, κι ἀνα-
τινάζεται, κι ὅλο στενεύει καί ρουφιέται. Χω-
ρίς ἦχο.

Ἐκεῖ θά περιμένουν ἄντρες τρυφεροί μέ κλά-
ματα. Καί τά μακριά μαλλιά τους ὄρθια στό
σκοτάδι, ὅπως τῶν πνιγμένων.

The Underground

In secret arcades, full of hanging bodies, weeds,
a hum like running water. So much water.

Behind the walls there's something creeping,
thick and huge, something already scorched by
hideous flames, perhaps a well, an under-
ground passage that explodes, contracting,
sucking in. Without a sound.

That is where tender men will wait in tears,
their long hair floating in the dark. The hair of
men who've drowned.

Τοῦ Κάτω Κόσμου

Ὡραῖα θηλυκά τοῦ Κάτω Κόσμου, μέ μακριούς ποδόγυρους κι ἐρεθισμένα μάτια. «Εὔμορφα, εὔμορφα!» τούς λέγαν καί τά στρίμωχναν. Ἀργότερα τά ἔκαναν τραγούδια. Διδακτικές γυναῖκες. Μέ λαιμά γεμάτα μελανιές. Μέ ζαρωμένα μεσοφόρια. Κι ἕνα φαρδύ, σάν φύλλο σκοτεινό, ματώνει στίς λινές τους βράκες.

Αὐτά νά μείνουν ἀπό τούς ἀρχαίους καημούς. Τούς ἔρωτες.

Of the Underworld

Beautiful ladies of the Underworld, with long hems and eyes sore from crying. "My fair ones!" they would call them as they cornered them. Later they turned them into songs. Exemplary ladies. With bruised necks. Crumpled petticoats. And on their linen pantalets, a stain of blood, a dark leaf, spreading.

Let that be what is left of ancient longings. And of ancient loves.

Τοῦ γάμου

Ὅπως στούς ὕπνους τῶν ἀγρίων καταποντίζε-
ται τό πλοῖο-φάντασμα, ἤ φαρμάκι τρώει τό
κύπελλο τοῦ ἀφέντη —μακριά ὁ δεμένος ρουθου-
νίζει σάν νά ξέφυγε, ἤ σάν λυμένος ἀπό χρόνια
καί μέ ὀόγχους— ἔτσι σοῦ μοιάζουν ὅλοι κομμα-
τιάζοντας, καί πάλι ἐσύ, κομμάτια ὅλοι.

Μέ κρότους καί μυστήρια φωνάγματα, μέ λι-
θοϐολισμούς καί ἀλληλούια κοιμοῦνται οἱ συ-
ζυγοκτόνοι.

The Wedding Song

Just as the phantom ship sinks in the sleep of savages, or poison cankers the master's cup— far off the captive moans, just escaped, perhaps untied for years and unaware—so they resemble you, torn to shreds, and you them, again, in pieces.

Through crashes and mysterious cries, stonings and alleluias, the spouse-killers sleep.

Οἱ κακοπαντρεμένες

Σάν ἀπό τά λυπητερά τραγούδια, καί διωγμέ-
νες μέ λυγμούς καί δόξασοι, μέ τά μακριά τά
κόκκινα καί τά ποδήρη, ψηλά ποδήματα τῶν
κυνηγιῶν, κι ὁ λόγος πανωπροίκι μαλακός καί
χορταριάζει, μέ φλόγες καί φρυάζοντας καί
γέλιο ἀκράτητο, νά μήν τόν δοῦν πού φοβερί-
ζει, φεύγουν—

ὅπως ἀστράφτει ὁ πετεινός στόν Ἅδη, κι ὅπως
χρυσή μασέλα στό βουβό τῆς νύχτας, τετράπο-
δο τρεχάτο πού κουδούνιζε, κι ὁ ἀναβάτης μά-
λαμα κοχλάζει.

The Unfortunate Brides

As in sad ballads, chased with sobs and glorias,
in dresses, long and red, and ankle-length, in
hunting boots, the dowry promised once, now
soft and moss-grown, with flames and fuming
and wild laughter, so they won't see him
threaten, they leave—

the way a rooster lights up Hades, or a gilded
jaw the speechless night, a beast jangling on the
run, and the rider bubbles up gold.

Τά πάθη τῆς ἀγάπης

Παντοῦ νερά, σάν τά φλαμανδικά τοπία πού
δέν περνάει φῶς ἤ ψάρι, κι ἀπό τά ἔγκατα φω-
νές, θούρια πολιορκητῶν, ραγίσματα, λαβω-
ματιές ἀπό τούς μέσους χρόνους, ὄψεις βαρβά-
ρων χρυσωμένες καί πονᾶνε.

Μέ τό λαγοῦτο σταυρωτά στό στῆθος, καί τό
καρφί στό μάτι, πέρα πέρα, ἄντρες γενναῖοι,
κόρη εὐγενική, καί γύρω μαίνονται φουσάτα—

Ὡραία ζωγραφιά καί πράσινη, πού θά τήν πῶ
τά πάθη τῆς ἀγάπης.

The Sufferings of Love

Let there be water, as in Flemish landscapes, so that no fish or light passes through, and from the depths, songs of besiegers, voices, cracks, medieval wounds, the gilded faces of barbarians—in pain.

Always a lute across the chest, a nail straight through the eye—the noblemen, the maiden, legions all around them raging.

A beautiful painting, so green, I shall call it "The Sufferings of Love."

Τά κελάρια

Τά σπίτια πού ἔφτιαχναν ἄλλοτε, ἔμεναν κούφια ἀπό κάτω, καί τούς χώρους ἐκείνους τούς ἔλεγαν τότε κελάρι. Ἐκεῖ μέσα φυλάγονταν διάφορα πράγματα: παλαιός ρουχισμός, ὑποδήματα, τιμαλφή καί ὡραῖα γυαλιά, παγερά νυφικά καί λευκώματα, ὑπολείμματα ἐπίπλων μέ δύσκολο ὄνομα, καί, συχνά, κάποια πρόσωπα πού πολύ ἀγαπήθηκαν. Στήν περίπτωση αὐτή τά φιλοῦσαν σφιχτά καί τά κλείδωναν, καί ἀμέσως μετά χτίζαν ὅλες τίς πόρτες, γιά νά μήν τίς ἀνοίξουν καί φύγουν.

Καί καθώς δέν ὑπῆρχε διέξοδος, καί οἱ τοῖχοι γερά μαγκωμένοι, ἐκρατοῦσαν καλά τῶν παλιῶν οἱ ἀγάπες καί τίς νόμιζαν ὅλοι γι' ἀθάνατες.

The Cellars

The houses they built in those days were left hollow underneath and they called the spaces cellars. They kept odd things in them: old clothes, shoes, jewels, beautiful glass, stiff wedding gowns and albums, bits of furniture with difficult names, and quite often some people they dearly loved. When this was the case, they kissed them hard and locked them in, and then quickly bricked up the doors so they couldn't open them and leave.

Since there wasn't an exit and the walls held tight, the old loves lasted well and everyone took them for immortal.

Οἱ ἄπιστοι

Ἄς μείνει ἀνεξήγητος τοῦτος ὁ χτύπος σέ
γοῦρνες χωσμένες καί σήραγγες, ὅπως δραπέ-
της στή λίμνη ξημέρωμα.

Μέ πένθη αἰώνων νά πνέουν οἱ ἄνεμοι, σέρνον-
τας τρόμους λαθραίων ἐρώτων, ἐγκόλπια,
μαύρους πλοκάμους, μικρά εὐσεβή ἀναθήματα,
νέους πού βράχηκαν μέχρι τό κόκαλο σέ μπόρα
αἰφνίδια, ὥρα ἑσπέρας.

Καί πολλοί ποταμοί παρασύροντας στέγες
ἀθλίων, ἀγγελίες μικρῶν ἀποστάσεων, προ-
τροπές, νουθεσίες καί ὅρκους, ἀσπασμούς, καί
τά κλάματα. Παρασύροντας κλίνες ἀπίστων
συζύγων, καί τίς ἄνανδρες λέξεις «λαχτάρα
μου».

The Unfaithful

Let the knock in the underground troughs and the tunnels remain unexplained, like the fugitive by the lake at dawn.

While winds heave with ages of sorrow, dragging fears of clandestine love, amulets, black locks, small, pious oblations, young men soaked to the bone by a sudden storm at dusk.

And many rivers carrying away the roofs of the wretched, messages that never went far, urgings, oaths, admonitions, embraces, and tears. Carrying away the beds of unfaithful spouses, and the unmanly words "I need you."

Ἡ ἀπαγωγή

Νά προσέχεις προπάντων τήν πόρτα, μισή βυθισμένη, μισή ἀνοιχτή μέ ἀντικλείδι, καί κρέμεται. Λογχοφόροι κρατοῦν τήν ἀντίπερα, καί ἀναίτιος γδοῦπος: ἡ κλαγγή σιδερένιων βρεφῶν πού ἁρπάχτηκαν μέσ' ἀπ' τήν κούνια, καί κοράσια δαγκώνουν τά σεντόνια μέ χάχανα.

Τά πνιχτά λιτανέματα φύλαξε, τίς μουγκές λειτουργίες, τά λιωμένα σκουτάρια, τούς νάρθηκες, τῶν ἁρμάτων τό δέος. Γιατί μόνος θ' ἀκοῦς τά γρυλίσματα, καί αὐτόν πού ἀγαπᾶς θά φοβᾶσαι.

The Abduction

Above all watch the door, half buried in the ground, half opened by a passkey, hanging. On the other side lancers have taken control, an unprompted thump: the clanging of iron-wrought infants snatched from their cribs, and the little girls bite on their sheets tittering.

Guard your silenced processions, mute litanies, bows and quivers, worn-out shields, dread of arms. Because all alone you'll hear the growling, and fear the one you love.

Οἱ ἀγαπημένοι

Θά σέ κεντοῦν μέ λόγχες νά ξυπνᾶς, τό στόμα
σφραγισμένο μέ κερί νά μή φωνάξεις, καί θά
σέ κρύβουν μέ βαριά ὑφάσματα καί μέ νερά,
στόν πάτο λιμνοθάλασσας ὅπου παφλάζουν
πάνδημα βασίλεια.

Ὅτι γραφτό οἱ ἀγαπημένοι νά σοῦ φανερώνον-
ται στίς ὧρες τῶν κατολισθήσεων, σιδηρόφρα-
κτοι, μέσ' ἀπό γοερούς συναγερμούς κωπηλα-
τώντας —πάμφωτο βαθυσκάφος στ' ἀνοιχτά,
καί πάνω του πυρπολητές θαλασσοπόροι.

The Loved Ones

They will poke you with lances so you wake, your mouth sealed with wax so you won't scream, and hide you covered in heavy fabric and water, at the bottom of a saltwater lake where populous kingdoms splash.

As it is written, those you love will appear to you during avalanches, ironclad, rowing between mournful alerts—a bathyscaph all lit up offshore, with fireship navigators on board.

Τά ἐνδύματα

Τά τεκμήρια ἔμεναν πάντοτε στοῦ φονέως τόν
κῆπο, ξεσκισμένα ἀπό τέλειο φάσγανο, σάν
προικιά βουλιαγμένα στά ἕλη, σάν νά τά
'σπειρε κάποιος ἀλόγιστα στό φευγιό του ἀπά-
νω. Πελερίνες, μετάξια καί δίμιτα, μέ τήν αἴ-
γλη πού ἔπρεπε τότε, χλιαρές ἀλλαξιές πού
ποτίστηκαν μυρωδιές καί θορύβους, ζιπουνάκια
λευκά καί στηθόπανα μ' ἀραιές μαχαιριές καί
φεστόνια, καί τά εὔθραυστα ἐκεῖνα ἐνδύματα
πού τά λέγαν τό πάλαι ποτέ καμιζόλες.

Ὀνειρώδεις οἱ θάνατοι, καί ὁ δράστης ἀθῶος.
Μ' ἕνα τραῦμα τυφλό, σάν παράθυρο πού πα-
τιόταν μονάχα τίς νύχτες.

The Garments

The evidence stayed in the murderer's garden forever, shredded by a perfect blade, like clothes from a dowry sunk in marshes, thoughtlessly sown by someone on the run. Velvet cloaks, silk and dimity, with the splendor of a bygone era, warm changes of clothing, saturated with smells and noises, white vests and corselets scattered with stabs and festoons, and those fragile garments they used to call camisoles.

Deaths are dreamlike, but the agent is innocent. And his wound like a window that only gets trespassed at night.

Οἱ δουτηχτές

Τά «πάρεξ νά σέ ἰδῶ, καλέ μου», τά κρυφομι-
λήματα, μές᾽ ἀπό δύσκολους καιρούς σωσμέ-
να λόγια τῶν ἐξορκισμῶν, τίς σιγανές πατη-
μασιές, τά ποιήματα, ἀπόπειρες ἀγνοουμένων
πρό πολλοῦ,

νά τ᾽ ἀνασύρεις ὅλα ἀπ᾽ τά δαθιά, ἀπό μεγά-
λα σκότη, ἀνέπαφα, ἀπ᾽ τίς σιωπές ἐρειπωμέ-
νων μητροπόλεων, τήν ἄλωση, τή θεομηνία,
τή ρομφαία: ὅπως τροπαιοφόρος δουτηχτής δα-
ραίνει στ᾽ ἄπατα, ἤ εὐπατρίδες πελεκᾶν τήν
ὥρια κόρη, κι ὁ πιό καλύτερος τῆς παίρνει τό
κεφάλι—

Γιά νά γυρνᾶς καί νά ᾽ρχεσαι καί νά μιλᾶς,
λόγια σπουδαίων εἰδυλλίων πού ἦταν μιά φο-
ρά, ἴχνη λαμπρῶν καρατομήσεων, τά «σέ φι-
λῶ», ἄχ πόσο σέ φιλῶ, τό δῆγμα ἐπίχρυσο,
ἐπιτέλους, ἀπ᾽ τό χρόνο.

The Divers

The "nothing, save to see you, my love,"
hushed conversations, the words to exorcisms
salvaged from difficult times, the quiet foot-
steps, poems, attempts of those missing for
ages,

you must dredge it all up from the depths, from
the great darkness, intact, from the silence of a
ruined metropolis, the fall, the plague, the flam-
ing sword: like the diver encumbered by his
prize in the bottomless sea, or patricians who
hack the fair maiden and the best takes her
head—

So that you will return and come over and talk,
words from great romances that happened long
ago, the traces of glorious beheadings, "with
kisses," yes with kisses, and the bite, at last,
gilded by time.

Γ΄
Τρία τραγούδια
γιά ὥρα μεγάλης ἀνάγκης

III
Three Songs
in Case of Emergency

Μαγικό ξόρκι νά σέ φυλάει ἀπό δάγκαμα
φιδιοῦ, κακό ἐχθρό,
καί ὅλα τά ἐπουλωμένα τραύματα

Πέντε μαῦρο ἑσπερινό, τρεῖς καί φτάσε δέσπο-
τα, δέκα μπρούντζινη κλωστή καί φοράδα κόκ-
κινη, μέ ἀνάποδο ἄνεμο πῶς θυμώνει τό νερό,
ἕξι στρίγκλες στό πηγάδι καί κουλός ὁ περα-
τάρης, πάνω κάτω στό μπουντρούμι ἕντεκα
χλωρές κυράδες, δεκατρεῖς καραβοκύρης κι
ἅγιος πρωτομάστορης, ἕνα καί στή σάπια
σκούνα θά τούς πνίξει ὁ γιός τοῦ δράκου.

**A magic spell to protect you from
snake bites, evil enemies,
and all the healed wounds**

Five for black vespers, three for the priest,
hurry to the church and arrive on time, ten for
the bronze thread, and for the red mare, how
the water maddens with a backward wind, six
for the witches next to the well, ferry them
across with his one arm lost, thirteen for the
shipper and again for the saint, up and down
the dungeon the eleven ladies pace, and one for
the son of the dragon sire, watch him, he will
drown them in a rotten skiff.

Ἐμβατήριο πού θά λένε οἱ τρελοί,
ὥρα νυχτερινή πού βγαίνουν περιπολία

Προέχουν ὅμως τά φτερά, καί οἱ πομπές τῶν
ὑπνοφόρων. Ἔλεος, ἔλεος ἀκαριαῖο, πέφτει
σφυρί στήν πέτρα καί ξεχύνεται.

Κίτρινο, κίτρινο ἀλογατάκι,
τοῦ στρατηλάτη τό φαρδύ πουκάμισο
πῶς μάκρυνε καί τρέμει.
Τό τέρας ἔχει σηκωθεῖ μ' ἑφτά πελέκια κι ἔρχεται.
Πίσω ἀπ' τίς πόρτες θά τροχίζουν ἀντρειωμένους.

**The march the madmen will chant
while making their nightly rounds**

First come the wings and the parades of sleepbearers.
Mercy, lethal mercy, the hammer strikes the stone and
overflows.

Yellow, yellow pony
the warlord's ample shirt
how it lengthens and trembles.
The beast has risen and is coming with seven axes.
Behind the doors they will sharpen the brave men like knives.

Μικρή ὠδή στόν Θεῖο Ἰούλιο,
γιά νά 'ρχεται τά βράδια σφυρίζοντας,
μ' ἕνα σβηστό φανάρι

Ἀνεξιχνίαστος θά μείνει ὁ πνιγμός, θηλιές
καί σεῖστρα, οἱ ναυτίλοι ὠχροί, κι οἱ ἄλλοι
γαλανοί σάν γίγαντες.

Καί ὅπως ὁ ταξιδευτής πού, ἐπιστρέφοντας,
βλέπει ἄξαφνα τό ἀερόστατο κι ἀνάβει, διά-
τρητο ἀπό βέλη ἀγρίων —ἔτσι νά φτάνεις ἀπό
τά νωπά μεσάνυχτα σέ τρομερές αὐλές καί σέ
χορτῶνες, νά 'ρχεσαι σάν ἀπό τά ξένα, καί
τρυπώντας τούς βρεγμένους τοίχους,

ἐντροπαλός, γιά νά σοῦ λέω ἱστορίες.

A short ode for Uncle Jules
so he'll come by at night whistling
with his lantern unlit

There is no way to trace the drowning, nooses,
and rattles, some sailors pale, and others blue
as giants.

And like the traveler who suddenly, on his way
home, sees his balloon catch fire, riddled by
savages' arrows—like him you will leave fresh
midnights for grand courtyards and meadows,
you will arrive as if from foreign lands, break-
ing through damp walls,

timid, so that I can tell you tales.

Δ´
Μικρές παράξενες ἱστορίες

IV
Strange Short Tales

Περί τῶν ἀφηγήσεων ἐν γένει

Τίς γραφές τους νά τρέμεις τίς ἄπατες κι ὅλο
πατήματα—

βιγλατόρων πού γέρνουν στήν ξύλινη γέφυρα,
κι ἀπό πέρα φωτιές κι ἐνορίες σφαγμένες, ἤ
φωνές ναυαγίων κι ἐκρήξεις, ἁρπαγές γυναι-
κῶν καί τό πλιάτσικο κεντρικῆς ἀγορᾶς ὅπου
ξέσπασε πυρκαγιά μεσημέρι, καί βουνά πού
χαράζονται, ὅπως γκρεμίζει πανάρχαιο ἰκρίω-
μα, ἤ κλαψούρισμα ζώου πού βρέθηκε νύχτα
στό ρέμα νά 'χει ἔξαφνα δύο κεφάλια—

Μέ φωνές στρατευμάτων σέ ὥρα ἐπίθεσης,
μουγκρητά καί ἀνάθεμα, μέ βαθιές βασκανίες
καί ξόρκια, μέ γητειές, μαγγανεῖες,

νά φυλάγεσαι, λέω, τούς αὐτόχειρες πού ἔγρα-
φαν.

About narratives in general

You must fear their bottomless scriptures that
echo with footsteps—

of sentrymen leaning over the wooden bridge,
and in the distance fires, the slaughtered parish,
or cries from shipwrecks and explosions, ab-
ducted women, and the looting of a market-
place ablaze at noon, and mountains scored, an
ancient scaffold ready to collapse, or late at
night, deep in some gully, the whimper of a
beast which found itself, all of a sudden, with
two heads—

With battle cries at the hour of attack, howls
and curses, with exorcisms and incantations,
hexes, charms,

I say beware the suicides who wrote.

Τόποι φλεγόμενοι καί πολιορκημένοι,
πού δέν ἔγιναν

Ἦχοι καταιγισμῶν κι ἄς μή σαλεύει τίποτα.
Μόνο τίς νύχτες νά σηκώνεται μαῦρος ἀέρας
καί νά βλέπεις: Πλῆθος μεγάλο καί ἀχνίζει κι
ἔρχεται, μέ μυτερά σκουφιά, σάν ἀπ' τούς πά-
γους, ἀλλά, μέ σιγανό μουκάνισμα κρυφομιλά-
νε καί νά σπρώχνονται.

Καί πίσω πίσω κρέμεται ἀνάποδα ὁ στραβοκά-
νης, πρησμένος ἀπό τ' ἀσημένια τάλιρα, καί
φτύνει.

**Lands besieged and in flames,
that never existed**

A distant rumbling. Nothing moves. When black winds rage after dark you see: a great crowd drawing near, steamy, with pointy hats, as if from icy places. They push each other grunting softly.

And further off the bandy-legged man hangs upside down, swollen with silver coins, and spits.

Ἀναπαράσταση σπανίου ἐθίμου:
χρώματα ἔντονα καί ἀπαθεῖς μορφές,
σάν μέσα σέ ἀκίνητο νερό

...καί τούς ἐτσάκιζαν καλά καλά γιά νά τούς
δώσουν σχῆμα ἀγγέλου, κι ἔπειτα τούς ἐξέθε-
ταν σέ τόπους ὀχυρούς καί σέ ἀλάνες, ὅπου μέ
σύναξη μεγάλη καί μυσταγωγία τούς γλυκο-
κουβεντιάζαν καί τούς φώναζαν. Ὥσπου μέ τά
πολλά Ὑπερυψοῦτε, γονυπετεῖς καί μεγαλεῖα,
σκεπάστηκαν οἱ θόλοι μέ νεκρούς ἱπτάμενους,
ἐξαρθρωμένα μέλη καί βαριά κατάγματα,
στάσεις μεγάλης ἀγωνίας, ἀλλά καί ὡραιότα-
τα φτερά, φωτάκια (πού τά ἔτρεμαν οἱ παλαι-
οί), ἀνθρώπινους τροχούς πού διάβαζαν τό μέλ-
λον —κεφάλια μέ ὀχτώ ποδάρια σάν βελόνια—
καί ἄλλα θαύματα, ὀδυνηρά καί ἀξιοθέατα.

Γιατί ἐκεῖνες τίς ἡμέρες, ὅπως λένε, ἔβγαιναν
κήρυκες μέ τό ψαλίδι καί λαλοῦσαν.

Depiction of a rare custom:
vivid colors and impassive faces,
as seen in still water

. . . and they would break their limbs giving
them the shape of angels, and then exhibit them
in fortified places, and in abandoned lots,
where with great assembly and secret rites they
would placate them, call them back. Until, with
all the holier-than-thous, genuflection, and
adoration, the domes covered over with flying
corpses, dislocated bones, and awful fractures,
postures of extreme agony, but also the most
beautiful wings, tiny lights (so dreaded back
then), human wheels that could tell the future
—heads with eight tentacles like needles—and
other wonders, harrowing but spectacular.

For, in those days, it is said, heralds appeared
with scissors and proclamations.

Τό ἀρχαιότατο ἐπάγγελμα τῶν γυρολόγων

Ἕναν καιρό, στά ὑπαίθρια παζάρια, συνέβαιναν τοῦ κόσμου τά θαυμάσια. Πετοῦσαν ἀπό τούς γκρεμνούς ὅλοι οἱ καμένοι, κι ἔφερναν φιαλίδια θολά, μυστηριώδη φονικά παρασκευάσματα, δόντια ἤ καδένες πού ἔχασαν οἱ ἄφρονες πηδώντας στό μεγάλο ρῆγμα, καί ὡρολόγια μέ τίς συνήθεις παραστάσεις: ὠχροντυμένες, μανιακούς, δαιμονισμένους.

Ἔλεγαν ὅμως καί τροπάρια μελωδικά, σέ γλώσσα μᾶλλον δυσανάγνωστη καί αὐστηρή, σάν κείμενο ἀνεπανόρθωτα φθαρμένο πού ὅλο πάει νά τραγουδήσει καί λυγίζει. Πῶς κράζει φτερωτό σκυλί, ἀδιάβατο πρωινό, χάσκει ψηλά τό στόμα του καί ξεματώνει.

The peddlers' ancient trade

Once upon a time in the marketplaces the most wondrous things happened. All the burned men flew out of abysses carrying cloudy phials, mysterious death potions, teeth, or pendants that the dreamers lost when they lept into the gorge, and watches with the usual scenes: pale-clad women, maniacs, possessed men.

But they were also chanting melodious hymns, in a rather indecipherable, and strict tongue, like a text irreparably worn, which is always about to sing, but falters. The way a winged dog howls, impenetrable dawn, its jaw wide open and bleeding.

Πῶς μίλησαν αὐτόπτες μάρτυρες, ψευδομανεῖς καί δεισιδαίμονες ἐπίσης

Εἶπαν καί γιά τόν σαλπιγκτή, πώς τάχα πρό-
καμε νά εἰδοποιήσει, κι ὅπου φύγει φύγει. Κι
ἔναν ἀκόμη, ὀνομαστικά, πώς τ' ὀνειρεύτηκε
ἀποβραδίς, ἤ μᾶλλον τό 'δε μέ τά μάτια του:
Πελώριο θηρίο, μετέωρο, φλεγόταν πάνω ἀπ'
τά νερά μέ ἀφρούς καί ὀλόλυζε, κι οἱ τοῖχοι
ἔφεγγαν καθώς ἀπό λεπτότατη διφθέρα, πα-
λαιική, μέ ἀμνημόνευτα χαράγματα. Καί πέ-
ρα, στά πολλά τά χώματα, εἶχε ξασπρίσει ἡ
γῆς κι ἀραίωνε, σάν τό ζυμάρι πού φασκιώνουν
τίς σαϊτιές, καί σάν ἀπ' τό ψιλούτσικο χαρτί
πού δένονται οἱ ἀστροκαμένοι κι οἱ ἐξωμότες.

What the eyewitnesses said,
all of them superstitious and compulsive liars

And they talked about the trumpeter as well,
and how he got there in time to warn, and then
ran off as quick as he could. And of someone
else, by name, who dreamed it all the night be-
fore, or rather saw it with his own eyes: A
Great Beast on fire, hovering above the water,
foaming and wailing, and the walls aglow as if
made of the finest vellum, antique, with im-
memorial marks. And way off, by a pile of dirt,
the earth so pale and thin, like the dough they
wrap wounds in, as fine as the paper that binds
the star-crossed and the apostates.

Ἀπό σπαράγματα βραχέος χρονικοῦ:
μεγάλος διωγμός, ἀγνώστου ἔτους,
ἀλλά προπάντων σέ ὡραία πόλη,
περίβλεπτη, μέ λιγοστές κρυψῶνες

Εὐλόγησον, ξεφωνητά, καί βουτηγμένοι στό
μετάξι νά δαγκώνουν τό βαρύ λεπίδι Μή Μι-
λᾶς

καί ἀσκεπεῖς καί ἐκδικούμενοι ψηλά ψηλά σέ
κορυφές ἀλόγων σάν ἀλλόφρονες, ἀπ' ὅλες τίς
μεριές μπουκάρουν φράζοντας, ὅπως αὐτός ὁ
βόμβος ἐπιμένει, ἤ πάλι σέρνοντας μνηστή δε-
μένη κι ἄλαλη, ὀνόματι

Πώς ἔφταιξαν πολλοί ἐκεῖνες τίς ἡμέρες, καί
πολλοί ματώνοντας

Fragments from a brief chronicle:
a great persecution, year unknown,
but more important, in a beautiful city,
conspicuous, with scant hiding places

Blessed Be, screams, and buried in silk, let them
bite the weighty blade Be Silent

Uncovered and full of revenge high up on
horses like mad men, they swarm from every
direction, closing in, the way this buzzing per-
sists, or again dragging a fiancée bound and
gagged, by the name of

For, in those days, many were to blame, and
many were bleeding

Διά χειρός ἀγνώστου, πραγματεία

Εἶναι, βεβαίως, μερικοί πού πυρπολήθηκαν διασχίζοντας κατεστραμμένο ὀρυχεῖο. Ἄλλοι λαμπάδιασαν βουτώντας ἀπό ἐξῶστες κεντρικῶν μεγάρων, καί ἄλλοι, τέλος, γίναν παρανάλωμα (πλέοντας ἀνοιχτά, μέ κάτι ἱστιοφόρα ἐπισφαλή, βρατσέρες ἴσως).

Κανείς δέν ξέρει τί νά γίνονται οἱ πλέον δυσεύρετοι, αὐτοί πού ὡς ἐλεεινοί κλεπταποδόχοι, αὐτόμολοι, κυκλοφοροῦν ἀνάμεσά μας. Λέγεται, ἁπλῶς, ὅτι θεῶνται στίς μεγαλουπόλεις, μέ τό ἔγκαυμα τώρα στιλπνό ἀπό τήν πάροδο τοῦ χρόνου. Δέν τό μιλοῦν, μά τό ἐπιδεικνύουν —σπανίως, εἶν' ἡ ἀλήθεια, ὅποτε τό καλεῖ ἡ ἀνάγκη— σάν βούλλα αὐτοκρατορικῆς ἐπιστολῆς πού ἐκλάπη καθ' ὁδόν, κακόπεσε, κι ἐνόσω ἀμέριμνος ὁ αὐτοκράτωρ γευματίζει, ὁ ταχυδρόμος του λιμνάζει στό βαθύ χωράφι καί βραδύνει.

Treatise, written by an unknown hand

Certainly there are those who caught fire as they picked their way through a wasted mine. And others who lit up like torches as they dove from balconies in the center of town, and still others who ended up in flames (drifting at sea in some sort of unsteady vessel, a brazzera perhaps).

No one knows what happened to those, hard to find, who circulate among us as miserable middlemen and deserters. It's simply noted that they have been seen in big cities, with their burn now shiny from the passage of time. They don't discuss it, but they show it—hardly ever, it's true, only when necessary—like a seal on an imperial missive, stolen en route, gone astray, and while the insouciant emperor dines, his postman lies in a deep field of blood and is late.

Τσοῦρμο κουρσάρων σέ παράλια βασιλεύουσα, πού χρόνους τήν πολέμαγαν ἀποκλεισμένη

Καί πέφτοντας ἡ πύλη, εἶδαν τότε ν' ἀστράφτουν σπάραχνα ἐξαίσιου κήτους, βαθυκύανα, καί πορφυρά σ' ἐκεῖνες τίς πτυχές ὅπου μονάχα ἐπαύλεις, συλημένοι τύμβοι, θρύμματα κάστρων ποντισμένα. Καί παρεκτός τά μέρη ὅπου δειπνοῦσαν οἱ πορνοβοσκοί, κανένας ἴσκιος, μήτε κάν αἰθάλη ἀπό καταυλισμό ἐπιζώντων, παρά μιά νηνεμία, ὅπως σέ πνιγερό λαγούμι τῶν μαστόρων πού κατεργάζονταν τά μελανά ὀρυκτά.

Καί μάντευαν, μόλις, τό πέρασμα καταδρομῶν, ὁδούς ἀλόγων, διαβάσεις πατημένες, καί ὅ,τι ἀπόμενε ἀπ' τούς ἀγρούς τῶν φτερωτῶν λεόντων, τίς κρῆνες, τά λιωμένα ὑπέρθυρα, τά πανδοχεῖα ὅπου κινδύνεψαν πολλές φορές οἱ ἀνώνυμοι.

**A band of pirates,
at last in a city by the sea,
after years of battle**

And when the gate gave way, they saw the gills of an exquisite cetacean glittering, dark blue, and crimson in the folds where only villas, pillaged graves, and the sunken rubble of castles once existed. And except for the spots where the panders dined, no shade, not even smoke from the survivors' camp, just a dead calm, as in the airless shaft where craftsmen worked the black ore.

And they could just make out the route of plunderers, the horse trails, trodden paths, and what remained of the Winged Lion fields, fountains, worn lintels, and inns where the nameless were imperiled time and time again.

Κατάλογος πεσόντων,
καί τά ὅσα πρόσθεσε ἐμπειρικός γιατρός

Τό σέλας, ὤ τό σέλας τῶν πληγῶν, ἀνθρώπων
πλῆθος λαμπαδηφορούντων, καί στίς νωπές
ρωγμές οἱ κραδασμοί, οἱ ἄτακτες ὑποχωρήσεις,
ἀραιά καί πού χαλκός, ρινίσματα σιδήρου.
Ὅμως, ἐπάνω ἀπό ἐλάχιστα κορμιά, ὁλοσχερῶς
ἀναλωμένα, τό πρόσωπο αἰωροῦνταν σκιάζον-
τας τό ἄδειο ροῦχο —μυστήριο μέγα, ὁλωσδιόλου
ἀνεξάρτητο ἀπό βαθμούς στρατιωτῶν ἤ τάξεις.

Οἱ ἐστεμμένοι πάλι, σάν πλωτοί, ἐφέροντο ἀκό-
μη τοῦ ὕψους ἀπ' τό πλῆγμα, κατάγυμνοι, καί
πού νά ξεχωρίζεις πιά νόμιμο ἄρχοντα, σφετερι-
στή, τύραννο, διάδοχο τοῦ θρόνου. Γιατί ἐκείνους
δέν τούς βρῆκε τό κακό καβάλα στό ἄλογο, μήτε
σέ φοβερή τειχομαχία, παρά σέ περιβόλι ἀπόμε-
ρο τούς πέτυχαν μέ βρόχους.

Κι ἔτσι τούς σέρνουν ἀπό τήν ἀγκάλη ὅπού εἶχαν
ξεχαστεῖ, κι ἐμπρός στήν ἄσωτη παιδίσκη κρί-
νονται.

**Casualty list,
and what the empirical doctor added**

The shimmer, oh the shimmer of the wounds, of a crowd bearing torches, and in fresh rifts, the tremors, the disorderly retreats, and scattered here and there iron filings, bronze. However, above a few bodies, utterly spent, the face hovered, shading the empty garment—a great mystery, entirely separate from army rank or order.

The crowned again, still in the air, suspended by the blow, stark naked, and how can you tell anymore the rightful ruler, usurper, tyrant, heir to the throne. Since death never befell them on horseback, nor in open battle, but in a secluded garden, they got them with nooses.

And like that they drag them from the arms where they've forgotten themselves, and in front of the profligate lass they are judged.

Καί τί ἀπέγινε ὁ δολοφονημένος

Ἄλλοι τόν θέλουν, χρόνους ἔπειτα, ἔπαρχο, νό-
θο παιδί μιᾶς παρακόρης· ρουφιάνο οἱ τρίτοι, νά
ὑπηρετεῖ δυσώνυμη μεγαλειότητα· καί κάποιοι
—πῶς διχάζονται ξανά οἱ γνῶμες— ὁπλουργό,
συλλέκτη πολυτίμων λίθων, ἀνατόμο, καί πάν-
τως χῆρο ἀπό γυναίκα πόρνη, ἐκπάγλου καλλο-
νῆς, σέ μιά ἐπιδημία πού ἔφεραν τά καραβάνια
ἐμπόρων.

Τό θύμα θά μεταναστεύει διαρκῶς: στό λίκνο νή-
πιου ἡγεμόνος ἤ στό ξέφωτο, ἐκεῖ πού μακελεύ-
ουν τόν φυγάδα, στό ἄντρο τῶν συμμοριτῶν,
στούς πατριῶτες πού τρυγοῦν κλεμμένο ἁμάξι
στή χαράδρα, στή μυστική ἑτοιμασία τοῦ ἐκδι-
κητῆ, στά φῶτα πόλης, ἐκθαμβωτικά ὕστερα
ἀπό ἐτῶν συσκότιση,

ἀπό παντοῦ, μέ πολλαπλές μεταμφιέσεις θά
περνᾶ, συστασιώτης, ἐραστής καί ποντοπόρος,
πανοῦργος κάπελας, αἰχμάλωτος ἀνιχνευτής,
μέ δανεικές ζωές ἀκόμη.

And what happened to the man
who was murdered

Years later some want him a prefect, others the maid's illegitimate son, and still others a pimp serving ignominious nobles; and a few—once again, how opinions differ—a swordsmith, a collector of precious stones, an anatomist and most certainly a widower whose harlot wife of astounding beauty died in an epidemic which the trade caravans brought over.

The victim will always be on the move: to the infant ruler's crib or the clearing with the butchered fugitive, to the robbers' den, the ravine where patriots loot a stolen carriage, to the avenger's secret preparation, to city lights that dazzle after years of blackout,

he'll travel all over under various disguises, fellow conspirator, lover and seafarer, wily innkeeper, captive explorer, with borrowed lives to spare.

Ἐκείνων πού πολύ ἐκράτησαν
καί δέ μιλοῦσαν

Θά ἐπιστρέφουν πάντοτε αὐτοί πού ἄδικα, σέ
χρόνους ἄλλους, λησμονήθηκαν. Ἀπό δρακόν-
των κοῖτες, θύρες ἅρπαγος, ἀπό τά παρεκκλήσια
τῶν ἀπείρων φόνων, μέ χαλασμένα πρόσωπα θά
ἐπιστρέφουν ὡς ναυμάχοι, ἑλόβιοι ἄλλοτε, μέ
σκοτεινή ἐνδυμασία αἱρετικοῦ ἤ ἐπίορκου, καί
στίς ἀνήλιαγες διόδους καίγοντας.

Ὅπως ἐπαίτης ὕπουλος πρό τῶν τειχῶν, καλύ-
πτει ἐπιμελῶς μέ τό μανδύα του πληγές πού ἄν-
θισαν, μέ κάποιο θαῦμα. Κι ὅπως ἀρχαῖος γεω-
μέτρης λάμνοντας, νεκρώνει πίσω του τεράστιες
ἐκτάσεις κι ἀναβλύζει.

**About those who really held out
and did not speak**

They are sure to return, those who in other
times were unjustly forgotten. From dragons'
beds, abductors' doors, from the chapels of
endless murders, with ruined faces they will re-
turn, sea warriors, once paludal, in the dark
guise of heretic or perjurer, combusting in sun-
less alleys.

Just as a devious beggar outside the walls, care-
fully mantles his wounds, which bloomed by
some miracle. And an ancient geometer dead-
ens behind him huge expanses with his oars and
wells up.

Ε΄
Τί ἔλεγε ἐκείνη ἡ ἐπιστολή

V
What that Missive Said

Μά ὅταν κάποιος σοῦ μιλᾶ μέ τρόμους, φωνές
χαμένων σέ ἀπαίσια σπήλαια καί βάλτους—

ἐσύ νά σκέφτεσαι προπάντων τί μπορεῖ νά ἐν-
νοεῖ, ποιό διαμελισμένο πτῶμα κρύβει στό ὑπό-
γειό του, τί δαγκωτά φιλιά καί φόνους, νύχτα
ὑπόκωφη, πού σιωπηλά τή διασχίζουν ἀμαξο-
στοιχίες (συσκοτισμένες μέ βαριά παραπετά-
σματα, καί στούς τροχούς πανιά ἤ βαμπάκι), τί
ἄνομες ἐπιθυμίες, λύσσα, ψιθύρους, οὐρλιαχτά,
βεγγαλικά σέ λάκκους πολιούχων, ἐκδικητές νά
τόν μουσκεύουν στό αἷμα ὅταν κοιμᾶται, ποιόν
κλέφτη, τέλος, σέ βαθύ κοιτώνα χάλκινο, πνιγ-
μένον στά λινά καί κλαίει—

καί νά τόν συμπαθεῖς, προπάντων νά τόν συμπα-
θεῖς, ἀγαπητέ Ἀρθοῦρε ἤ Ἀλφόνσε.

But when someone talks to you with terror, with voices of those lost in ghastly caves and marshes—

above all you must consider what he might mean, what dismembered corpse he is hiding in his cellar, what biting kisses, murders, muffled nights, crossed noiselessly by trains (darkened by heavy curtains, with rags and cotton round the wheels), what iniquitous desires, rage, murmuring, howls, fireworks by the patrons' tombs, avengers who soak him in blood while he sleeps, what thief, finally, in a deep, brass bedchamber, smothered in linen, and cries—

and you must feel for him, above all feel for him, my dear Arthur or Alphonse.

ΜΑΡΙΑ ΛΑΪΝΑ

ΔΙΚΟ ΤΗΣ

ΤΥΠΟΓΡΑΦΕΙΟ «ΚΕΙΜΕΝΑ» 1985

Σ' ὅλες τὶς πράξεις γύρευε τὸν ἑαυτό της·
κανεὶς δὲν πρέπει νὰ τῆς ἔχει ἐμπιστοσύνη.

Hers

by Maria Laina

In everything she did she sought herself;
no one should trust her

Τοιχογραφία

Σώζεται ἡ ἀρχὴ ἀπ' τοὺς μηρούς
σὲ ἄτονο γαλάζιο
τμῆμα ποδιοῦ ἀκόσμητο πρὸς τὰ ἀριστερὰ
καὶ τμῆμα ἀπολήξεως φορέματος.
Στὸ δέρμα διακρίνονται γραμμὲς
κυρίως ὀξυκόρυφες.
Ὁ χῶρος τοῦ λαιμοῦ διακόπτεται
ἀπ' τὸν ἀριστερὸ βραχίονα
ποὺ φέρεται πρὸς τὰ ἐπάνω
ἐνῶ μονάχα τὸ δεξὶ στῆθος δηλώνεται
μὲ ἐλαφρὰ καμπύλωση.
Ἀπὸ τὸ κάτω μέρος τοῦ προσώπου
λείπει τὸ μεγαλύτερο κομμάτι.
Κόκκινα τρίγωνα ἢ τόξα
σ' ὅλο τὸ ἄσπρο τοῦ βολβοῦ.
Σώζεται ἐπίσης ἡ κορδέλα τῶν μαλλιῶν
καὶ ἡ στροφὴ τοῦ σώματος
ποὺ ἀσφαλῶς προϋποθέτει
ἀνάλογες κινήσεις τῶν χεριῶν.

Λείπει τὸ ἔδαφος τοῦ ἔρωτα.

Fresco

The beginning of the thighs remains
a dull blue
to the left a section of foot unadorned
and a section from the hem of the dress.
On the skin lines are visible
mainly sharp angles.
The neck area is interrupted
by the left arm
which is raised up
while only the right breast is registered
by a slight curve.
Most of the lower part
of the face is missing.
Red triangles or arcs
cover the white of the eye.
The hair ribbon also remains
and the body's twist
which surely presupposes
similar movements in the hands.

The ground of love is missing.

1

Ἡ Μαρία μέσα στὸν καθρέφτη
ὁλόσωμη
στρώνει τὸ φόρεμά της στὸ λαιμό.
Δὲν ἔχει σημασία τώρα ποῦ ξαπλώνει τὸ κορμί της
ἂν ἔγινε σημύδα ἢ χορτάρι
ἡ Μαρία μέσα στὸν καθρέφτη
στρώνει τὸ φόρεμά της στὸ λαιμό.

Maria in the mirror
full-length
straightens her dress at the neck.
It does not matter now where her body lies
whether she turned to birch or grass
Maria in the mirror
straightens her dress at the neck.

Τριμμένο μὲ νερὸ καὶ στάχτη παρελθόν.
Ἡ Μαρία γελάει
γυρίζει καί ξαναπαίρνει τὴ θέση της.

Ἀντικριστὰ ὁ ἴασπις κι ὁ ἴασμος

The past scrubbed with water and ashes.
Maria laughs
turns and takes her place again.

Jasper and jasmine opposed

Δὲν εἶναι ἐδῶ
οὔτε ἄλλοτε·
ἄλλοτε ἦταν.
Ὁ ἔρωτας εἶναι ἀλλοῦ
καὶ μόνη της
δὲν ἦταν ποτέ.

She is not here
nor was she;
once she was.
Love is elsewhere
and never was she
alone.

Ἡ Μαρία στέκεται
σωπαίνει ἀμίλητη.

Ὡραῖο φῶς τῆς μέρας.

Maria stands
grows silent.

Fair daylight.

Ἡ ὕπαρξη στὸν ἴδιο χῶρο
δύο ὁλόβαφων τριγώνων
καὶ δίπλα τους νὰ διακρίνεται ἡ ἀρχὴ
κίτρινου χρώματος
τὴν ἄφηνε ἀδιάφορη·
ἀφοῦ καὶ νὰ μισεῖ μποροῦσε
κατὰ τὸν ἴδιο τρόπο ποὺ ἀφοσιώνεται στὸ κέντημα.

The existence in the same area
of two solid color triangles
and next to them the beginning
of a yellow color
left her indifferent;
since she could also hate
the same way she devoted herself to needlework.

Καθὼς μεγαλώνει
ἀναχωρεῖ μὲ περισσότερη ἄνεση.

Ἴσως καὶ κάποια ἕλξη.

As she grows older
she departs with greater ease.

Perhaps even allure.

Δὲν ἔχει τίποτα νὰ πεῖ.
Πιάνεται μόνο
καὶ κοιτάζεται
καὶ θέλει

She has nothing to say.
She simply touches herself
and watches herself
and wants

Ἐνῶ ὁλόκληρες φράσεις περνοῦν καὶ τὶς δέχεται
καὶ διατρέχει συνεχῶς μεγάλο κίνδυνο
ἀκόμα τὸ κορμὶ ποὺ θυμόταν
ἀλλὰ ὑπῆρχε κάτι ποὺ δὲν εἶχε ξαναδεῖ.

While whole phrases pass by and she accepts them
and she constantly faces great danger
still the body she remembered
but there was something she had never seen.

Ὡραῖα· κι ἂς εἶναι θλιβερὸ
γιατὶ δὲν παύει νά 'ναι ὡς τὰ σήμερα
νὰ σκύβει πάνω ἀπ' τὸ κορμί της
καὶ ν' ἀνασαίνει μὲ φωνές.

Ἔπειτα εἶναι μόνη της·
δὲν ἐμπιστεύεται κανέναν ὅταν λέει
χαϊδεύω τὸ κορμί μου
χαϊδεύω τὸ ἀδέξιο σῶμα μου.

Ὄχι πῶς ἔχει σημασία·
λίγο τὴ νοιάζει
γιατὶ χρυσὸ ἐλάφι στὴν κοιλάδα
ὀνειρευόταν νὰ ξαπλώνει.

Fine; even if sad
since until now it has never ceased being
leaning over her body
and breathing with voices.

Then she is alone;
she trusts no one when she says
I caress my body
I caress my awkward body.

Not that it matters;
she hardly minds
because she dreamt herself lying down
a golden deer in the valley.

2

Δὲν ὑπάρχει καμιὰ ἀμφιβολία.
Καὶ ἡ κατεύθυνση
καὶ ὁ προορισμὸς
(μετωπικὸς κι ἀφύσικος)
τὸ μαρτυροῦν.
Λίθινο βέβαια
ἀναθηματικό.

There is no doubt.
Both the direction
and the inclination
(frontal and unnatural)
prove it.
Stone, of course
anathematic.

Ὅταν ἄρχισε νὰ θυμᾶται
ἦταν καλοκαίρι
δὲν ὑπῆρχε ἄλλος
κι ἔπαιρνε μόνο ὅ,τι ἤθελε.

When she began to remember
it was summer;
no one else existed
and she took only what she wanted.

Στρώνει ἕνα κρεβάτι ἄδειο
ἥσυχα μελετάει τὴν ἀπόφασή της
μέσα στὸ φῶς.

She makes an empty bed;
calmly she contemplates her decision
in the light.

Ἐπειδὴ ἀπόψε
περνοῦσε μὲ ἅμαξα μπροστὰ στὸ καλοκαίρι
κι ἔνιωθε τὴν ἀνάγκη νὰ ξεχάσει
ὅτι στὰ ὄνειρά της ἦταν πάντα ἕνα δέντρο
ἕνα ἀπ' τὰ πολλὰ
γεμάτη δάκρυα
καὶ τώρα ἐπιστρέφει.

Because tonight
she passed before summer in a carriage
and felt the need to forget
that in her dreams she was always a tree
one in many
full of tears
and now she returns.

Μὲ ρὸζ ὀμπρέλα κάποτε
διέσχιζε τὸν ψίθυρο καὶ τὴ σιωπὴ

Once with a pink umbrella
she walked across the whispers and silence

Ἡ Μαρία μπροστά της
μὲ βουτηγμένο τὸ κορμὶ ὡς τὴ μέση.
Ἂν ἀποφάσιζε νὰ μείνει ἢ νὰ φύγει
ἦταν ἐκεῖ.

Maria in front of her
in up to her waist.
Whether she decided to stay or leave
she was there.

Ἕνας ὑπαινιγμὸς γιὰ κείνη
θὰ καταλήξει στὴ μελαγχολία
ὄχι γιατὶ θὰ πέφτει μαλακὰ τὸ βράδυ
ἀλλὰ γιατὶ πληγώνεται γιὰ χάρη της ἀκόμα.

Βγαίνοντας ἀπὸ τὴν πλαγιὰ στὸ δρόμο
προσπάθησε νὰ μὴν προσέχει τὴ σιωπή.

A hint of her
will end in melancholy
not because night will fall softly
but because she is still in pain for her sake.

Coming off the slope onto the road
she tried not to notice the silence.

Χαμογελάει τὶς περισσότερες φορές.
Αὐτὴ ἡ Μαρία
ἀπὸ τὴν ἄποψη αὐτὴ—

Most times she smiles.
This Maria
from this perspective—

3

Δὲν μπορεῖ νὰ ἀποδοθεῖ σὲ κανέναν
κι αὐτὸ τὸ ξέρει ἄθελά της.

She cannot be attributed to anyone
and she knows it unwittingly.

Εἶχε μπλεχτεῖ στὸ νόημα
μιᾶς ἄκαιρης λέξης
— τί σημασία ἔχει πιά ;
Ὅταν γεμάτη φόβο καὶ λύπη
γύρισε νὰ κοιτάξει τοὺς ἄλλους
ἡ λέξη μεγάλωσε.

She had become tangled in the meaning
of an untimely word
—what does it matter now?
When full of fear and sadness
she turned to look at the others
the word grew larger.

Κάθεται, κι ἀνάμεσα σ' αὐτὴν δὲν ὑπάρχει
πρώτη φορὰ δὲν ὑπάρχει·
γιὰ ποιὸ λόγο πρέπει ν' ἀπαντήσει;

Θυμᾶμαι εἶπε κάτι γιὰ τ' ἀπόγευμα
κι ἔμεινε στὴν κατάσταση αὐτὴ
χωρὶς ν' ἀλλάξει θέση.

She sits, and between her she does not exist
for the first time she does not exist;
why should she answer?

I remember she said something about the afternoon
and remained in that state
without changing positions.

Πίνει ἕνα φλιτζάνι τσάι
καὶ χαίρεται
νὰ ἀνάβει ἕνα τσιγάρο.
Δὲ θὰ γεράσει ἥσυχα.

She drinks a cup of tea
and gets pleasure
from lighting a cigarette.
She will not grow old calmly.

Νὰ ζεῖ
ν' ἀπολαμβάνει μιὰ γεμάτη μέρα
νὰ κλείνει τὸ παράθυρο, ἀλλιῶς
τί ἄξιζαν οἱ μαγικές της ἱκανότητες.

To live
to enjoy a full day
to close the window, otherwise
what was her magic worth?

Στέκεται μὲ τὴν πλάτη στὸ παράθυρο·
τὸ βάζο
ἡ πρόθεση τῶν λουλουδιῶν.
Λέει στὸν ἀμαξὰ νὰ περιμένει.

She stands with her back to the window;
the vase
the intention of flowers.
She tells the coachman to wait.

Τὸ φῶς καὶ ἡ σκιὰ θὰ ἀντιγράφονται
χωρὶς καμία ἔμπνευση
μὲ ἀποτέλεσμα νὰ γίνει ἀφηρημένη·
ἄ, ἐπιτέλους, θά 'βλεπε τὸ τέλος.

The light and shade will be copied
without any inspiration
so that she becomes abstract;
ah, at last, she would see the end.

νὰ φορέσει τὰ ροῦχα της
νὰ χτενίσει τὰ μαλλιά της
νὰ βγεῖ στὸ δρόμο
νὰ περάσει ἀπέναντι

to wear her clothes
to comb her hair
to go out on the street
to cross over

Ἦρθε κοντά του τρέμοντας
ὥσπου φτάνει, φτάνει
κι ἂς πεθάνει καθένας μόνος του.

She came close to him trembling
until enough, enough
just let each of us die alone.

Τρία ὁλόκληρα λεπτὰ προτοῦ οὐρλιάξει—
Καθισμένη στὸ κίτρινο φῶς
ἑνὸς προχωρημένου ἀπογεύματος
οἱ θάμνοι χρυσοὶ
ὅ,τι δὲν ἀγαποῦσε ἔλειπε
ἔμειν᾽ ἐκεῖ ἀκίνητη
τρία ὁλόκληρα λεπτὰ προτοῦ οὐρλιάξει.
Ὅταν τὴν ταρακούνησαν ἀπάντησε:
Τὴν ἑπόμενη φορὰ
θὰ μποροῦσα νὰ μιλήσω μὲ κάποιον
καὶ ν᾽ ἀγαπήσω, ἂν χρειαστεῖ.

Three whole minutes before she howled—
Seated in the yellow light
of an advancing afternoon
the bushes were golden
what she did not love was missing
she stayed there motionless
three whole minutes before she howled.
When they shook her she replied:
Next time
I will be able to talk with someone
and to love, if necessary.

4

Εἶχε ξεχάσει·
οἱ ἄλλοι ὅλοι θὰ κοιμοῦνται
ἐνῶ αὐτὴ
τρελὰ λόγια ψιθυρίζει στὸν καθρέφτη της.

She had forgotten;
the others will be sleeping
while she
whispers crazy words in her mirror.

Λοιπὸν
ἡ Μαρία
ὅταν κανεὶς δὲν τὴν προσέχει
ταχτοποιεῖ τὰ χέρια της.

So
Maria
when no one is watching her
arranges her hands.

Δὲ θέλει ἀκόμα νὰ γυρίσει·
σηκώθηκε ἁπλῶς γιατὶ εἶναι τόσο ὄμορφα
κι οἱ μέρες μεγαλώνουν.

She does not want to return yet;
she got up simply because it's so beautiful
and the days grow longer.

Τὴν πῆγαν εὔκολα στὸ αὐτοκίνητο
καὶ βγαίνοντας ἀπὸ τὴν πόλη ἤξερε
ὅτι θὰ πάρει τὴ μορφὴ
ποὺ τώρα ἔχει γιὰ πάντα.
Ἀνοίγει λοιπὸν τὴ βεντάλια της.

They got her into the car easily
and as she left the city she knew
that she would take the shape
she now has forever.
So she unfolds her fan.

Εἶναι πολὺ εὐτυχισμένη ἐδῶ
κάθεται καὶ κοιτάζει καὶ
ὅταν ὁ ἥλιος παίρνει τὸ δωμάτιο
βλέπει καλὰ τὶς ὧρες νὰ περνοῦν.
Δὲ συμμετέχει
διαβάζω ὅμως καὶ
κοιμᾶμαι ἥσυχα τὰ βράδια.
Σκέφτομαι, καμιὰ φορὰ πετύχαινα γραμμὲς
σχεδὸν μὲ μονοκοντυλιά.

She is very happy here
she sits and stares
when the sun fills the room
she watches closely the hours passing.
She does not participate
I read however and
sleep calmly at night.
I think, sometimes I managed lines
in one pencil stroke.

Ξάπλωνε μὲ τὰ μάτια ἀνοιχτὰ
κανένας δὲν κατάλαβε ὅτι δὲν ἤτανε αὐτή.

She lay down with her eyes wide open
no one understood that it was not her.

5

Δὲν ἔκρυβε τὴν ἔκπληξή της.
Σ' ὅλη της τὴ ζωὴ ἦταν εὐτυχισμένη·
γιατὶ ἂν θέλησε νὰ βρεῖ δικαιολογίες
δὲν εἶχε καμιά.

She did not hide her surprise.
All through her life she was happy;
because if she wanted to find excuses
she had none.

Παρέσυρε μαζί της
καὶ τὰ πουλιά ἀπ' τὸ χαλὶ
κι ὕστερα βγῆκε
χωρὶς ἀγκῶνες
χωρὶς γόνατα.

She even dragged with her
the birds from the rug
and then she left
without elbows
or knees.

Ἐκεῖ, ψιθύρισε
ἐκεῖ τὴν ἔβλεπα τὴ θάλασσα.

There, she whispered
there, I could see the sea.

Ἀπὸ τὴν πρώτη κιόλας ἐπαφὴ
δὲν παρουσίασε ἀντίσταση·
ὁλόκληρο τὸ κορμί της εὐφραινόταν.
Παρέδωσε λοιπὸν στὶς στάχτες
ὅ,τι ἀπόμενε ὀρθὸ
κάηκαν ὅλα, τότε.
Τὴν ἴδια μοίρα γνώρισε
κι ὁ πρωινὸς περίπατος.

From the very first touch
she did not resist;
her whole body rejoiced.
She consigned to the ashes
whatever was left
everything burned, then.
Even the morning stroll
came to a similar fate.

Φόρεσε τὸ κασκόλ της
ἔσβησε τὸ φῶς
ἐδῶ καὶ ἔξι νύχτες πεθαμένη
προσέχοντας μὴν ξεχαστεῖ
σὲ κάτι τόσο εὔθραυστο
βγῆκε στὸ δρόμο
καὶ μπροστὰ στὰ μάτια της
τὴν τίναξε
πρὶν ἀπὸ πόσα χρόνια τώρα
ὁ πρωινὸς ἀέρας.

She put on her scarf
turned off the light
dead for six nights now
careful not to lose herself
in something so fragile
she went out into the street
and in front of her eyes
how many years ago now?
the morning wind
jolted her.

Δὲν εἶχε σκοτεινιάσει ἀκόμα
κι ἴσως πραγματικὰ νὰ ἦταν
μέσα στὰ σάλια καὶ τὸ γέλιο της
ἀνόητη, ἀλλὰ
δὲν εἶχε σκοτεινιάσει ἀκόμα
ὅταν ἕνα βαθὺ φτερὸ
πέρασε ἀπ' τὰ μάτια της
ἕνα μελίσσι μὲ φωνές.

It had not gotten dark yet
and perhaps she really was
in all her spittle and laughter
a fool, but
it had not gotten dark yet
when a deep wing
passed before her eyes
a swarm with voices.

Τὸ ἀπόγευμα
ἐνῶ ἡ πόλη ἦταν χαμηλὰ
ἡ Μαρία κατέλαβε ὁλόκληρο τὸ σῶμα της.

In the afternoon
while the city was down low
Maria took over her whole body.

6

Στὴ μέση ἑνὸς ἔξοχου κύκλου
ἀπὸ μεστὰ νοήματα
ἡ Μαρία στάθηκε
καὶ βγῆκε στὴ φωτογραφία
σιγανά
φτιάχνοντας τὴ φουρκέτα στὰ μαλλιά της.

Ἐκθαμβωτικὸς ἀέρας
φυσοῦσε τὴν ἀδιαφορία της.

In the middle of an exquisite circle
ripe with meaning
Maria stood
and appeared in the photograph
calmly
fixing the pin in her hair.

A dazzling wind
blew at her indifference.

Γδύθηκε στὸ σκοτάδι
πλάι στὰ φλιτζανάκια τοῦ καφὲ
καὶ τὸ καλὸ τραπεζομάντιλο.

'Εντελῶς ἄλλα λόγια σκεφτόταν.

She undressed in the dark
next to the coffee cups
and the best tablecloth.

She was thinking totally different words.

Σχεδίασε μὲ τὴ φωνή της ἕνα ψέμα·
ἡ Μαρία στὸν χλιαρὸ ἥλιο
σὲ βάζα ἀπὸ σμάλτο
ψιθυριστά.

She made up a lie with her voice;
Maria in the tepid sun
in vases of enamel
whispering.

Χρησιμοποίησε τὴ μέρα της ἁπλὰ
καὶ δὲ χρησίμευε σὲ τίποτα

She used her day simply
and she was of no use

Κρατοῦσε σοβαρὴ τὸ σῶμα της
στὸ χόλ, στὸ δρόμο
ἀνάμεσα σὲ ἄλλους.
"Εβλεπε πράγματα νὰ μεγαλώνουν·
μήπως μιὰ ἄλλη ποὺ κοιτάζει ἔξω;

'Εκεῖ ἔξω
ἔξω ἀπ' τὸ ἄσπρο της πρόσωπο
δυνάμωσε χωρὶς νὰ προσέξει
ὅτι γινόταν ὄμορφη.

Serious, she held her body
in the hall, in the street
in the midst of others.
She saw things grow;
could it be someone else staring out?

Out there
outside her white face
she grew strong without noticing
that she was becoming beautiful.

'Από τὴ μιὰ στιγμὴ στὴν ἄλλη
ἔπεφτε ἔξω καὶ τῆς ἄρεσε
ἀλλὰ αὐτὸ δὲν τὴν ἀπασχολοῦσε τώρα πιὰ
ἂν καὶ παρέμεινε εὐδιάκριτη
νὰ ἀπαντάει καὶ νὰ ἔρχεται.

Μήπως μιὰ ἄλλη ποὺ κοιτάζει ἔξω;

From one minute to the next
she fell out of line and liked it
but this no longer concerned her
though she could still be seen
answering and approaching.

Could it be someone else staring out?

Ἔπεσε ἀπ' τὸ σῶμα της
κύλησε μαλακὰ πάνω στὸ χιόνι
ἀπὸ μέρα σὲ μέρα·
ἴσως ὑπάρχει ἕνα τέτοιο μέρος, σκέφτηκε
ἀλλὰ παλιὸ καὶ ἥσυχο
καθόλου πειρασμὸς
καθόλου ἔρωτας.
Χαμήλωσε λοιπὸν τὴ βεντάλια της.

She fell out of her body
and rolled softly on top of the snow
from day to day;
perhaps a place like this exists, she thought
but old and quiet
no temptation
no love.
So she lowered her fan.

7

Ἡ Μαρία πέρασε καὶ κάθισε
ἔστρωσε ἥσυχα τὸ φόρεμά της
χωρὶς ν' ἀγαπάει
χωρὶς τὴν ἔξαψη νὰ πληγωθεῖ
περιεργάστηκε τὶς ἐποχὲς στὸ χιόνι
κι ἔδιωξε ἁπαλὰ τὴ μνήμη ἀπὸ τὸ στόμα της.

Κάθε λίγα βήματα
προχωροῦσε τὸ σούρουπο.

Maria came in and sat down
she slowly straightened her dress
without loving
without the heat of being hurt
she contemplated the seasons in the snow
and gently chased the memory from her mouth.

Every few steps
dusk advanced.

Φτιάχνει ἕναν κύκλο
ἕναν μικρότερο
ἕναν ἀκόμα πιὸ μικρό.

Οὔτε μιὰ φορὰ ἀπὸ τότε
δὲ θά 'ναι ἐκεῖ ν' ἀκούσει.
Τί; εἶπε
πρὶν προχωρήσει στὸ ποτάμι.

She makes a circle
a smaller one
an even smaller one.

She won' t be there to hear
not once since then.
What? she said
before she stepped into the stream.

ἄλλωστε στὴν ἀφήγηση αὐτὴ
φαίνεται ἡ ἀδυναμία
νὰ βρεθεῖ ἕνας χῶρος

besides in this narrative
the difficulty
of finding a space is clear

Ἡ Μαρία μόνη της
ἀκουμπισμένη σὲ θαμπὴ βροχὴ
οἱ φούξιες φορτωμένες ἄνθη.
Τὸ τελευταῖο πράγμα ποὺ συγκράτησε
πιὸ χαμηλὰ
λιγάκι δεξιότερα...

Maria alone
leaning on turbid rain
the fuchsias loaded with blossoms.
The last thing she remembered
a little lower
a little to the right . . .

Ἔσκυβε νὰ σηκώσει τὴ ζακέτα της
μὲ φόντο ἄλλοτε τὸ δάσος
κι ἄλλοτε τὶς καρέκλες στὴν παλιά τους θέση.
Παρμένη ὅμως ἀπὸ χαμηλὰ
καὶ μ' ἕναν ἀκαθόριστο ἀέρα.
Τοὺς δυὸ αἰῶνες ποὺ ἀκολούθησαν
ἀγνόησε τὸ μέταλλο καὶ τὸ μπαμπάκι
κι ἀπλώθηκε νοτιοανατολικά.

She was leaning over to pick up her jacket
sometimes against a forest background
sometimes with the chairs in their old position.
Taken however from below
and with an undefined air.
In the two centuries that followed
she ignored metal and cotton
and spread out southeastward.

8

Παρ' ὅτι δὲν ἐξιχνιάζει τίποτα
πλημμύριζε τὰ πεζοδρόμια
καὶ φύτρωνε

Even though she solves nothing
she flooded the sidewalks
and sprouted

Στὴν καλύτερη μορφή της
παρέμεινε ἀτάραχη
ἐνῶ τὸ σῶμα ἔγερνε μὲ μιὰ χαριτωμένη κίνηση

Toward her most perfect figure
she remained untroubled
while her body bent with a charming motion

Ἕνα παιχνίδι τοῦ φωτὸς
ὅπως ὅλοι μας τέλος πάντων

A game of light
like all of us after all

Δὲ σκέφτεται νὰ δεῖ κανέναν·
μάλιστα τὶς περισσότερες φορὲς
ὁ ἔρωτάς της ἦταν ἄτυχος

She does not think of seeing anyone;
besides most of the time
her love failed

Θὰ κάθεται λοιπὸν
ἢ εἶναι ξαπλωμένη

So she may be sitting
or she is lying down

Πολύ ἀργότερα
πέρασε ἕνα βαθυγάλαζο λιοντάρι
κι ἐκείνη φόρεσε τὸ σάλι της

Much later
a deep blue lion passed
and she put on her shawl

Ἐπικαλέστηκε τὸ ὄνομά της
κι ἀνασηκώθηκε σὲ ἄλλη ἐποχή.

She invoked her name
and was lifted into another era.

Ἐπίλογος

Epilogue

Εἶμαι στὴν ἀρχὴ τῆς ζωῆς μου καὶ εἶμαι ἔξω στὸ φῶς. Ἔχουν περάσει χρόνια ἀπὸ τότε καὶ προσπαθῶ νὰ ρουφήξω τὸ ἄσπρο. Μόνο τὸ φῶς χρειαζόμουν. Ὕστερα, σκέφτηκα, θὰ σταματήσω νὰ κάνω αὐτὸν τὸ θόρυβο. Ἄν σταματήσω νὰ κάνω αὐτὸν τὸ θόρυβο, θ' ἀκούσω κάτι πολὺ ὄμορφο. Δὲν ξέρω ἀκόμα, ἀλλὰ εἶμαι σίγουρη, κι αὐτὸ μοῦ συμβαίνει συχνά. Μοῦ συμβαίνει συχνὰ ἐκεῖ ποὺ κάθομαι καὶ σκέφτομαι, ἀλλὰ δὲν εἶναι καθόλου αὐτό. Καθόλου κάτι ποὺ σκέφτομαι, ἀλλ' αὐτὸ μὲ βοηθάει. Μὲ βοηθάει νὰ μὴν ἔχω τὸ νοῦ μου, νὰ μὴν περιμένω τίποτα. Γιατὶ τότε τίποτα δὲ θὰ μποροῦσε νὰ συμβεῖ, ἐκτὸς ἀπὸ κάτι ποὺ ἤδη τὸ ξέρω. Καὶ τί ξέρω ἐγώ; Τί ξέρω;

I am at the beginning of my life and I am out in the light. Many years have passed since then and I am trying to suck in the white. I only needed light. Later, I thought, I will stop making that noise. If I stop making that noise, I will hear something very beautiful. I do not know yet, but I am certain, and that happens to me often. It happens to me often when I sit and think, but it is not at all that. Not at all something which I think, but it helps. It helps if my mind is elsewhere, if I am not waiting for anything. Because then nothing can happen, except for something I already know. And me, what do I know? What do I know?

NOTES TO THE POEMS

The Cake

Page 7: Traditionally in many parts of Greece a cock is slaughtered and the blood poured onto the foundations when a new house is built.

Page 9: "Your shadow is walking across the wall as you cross the pan; an empty pan, and you, difficult to grasp, move across it." In the original, the confusion this phrase expresses is compounded not only by the repetition of the verb "to move across," but also by broken syntax and double meanings. The word ασύλληπτη means both inconceivable in the metaphorical sense of "difficult to grasp," but also "unable to conceive."

Page 13: The hunter is preparing a traditional Greek dish called *stifado*, which entails slowly cooking onions and rabbit in a tomato sauce.

Page 33: The reference in this poem and the next is to early Christian reliefs in which a fight between the bird and the snake symbolizes the fight between good and evil.

Page 35: "A Roman marble relief." See note to page 33.

Page 41: "the ostrich in that film." The reference is to Luis Buñuel's film *Phantom of Freedom* (1974).

Page 43: There are various references to Ariadne in this text, especially to the thread she uses to help Theseus find his way out of the labyrinth after he slays the minotaur.

Page 53: The marquis is the French author the marquis de Sade (1740–1814).

Page 53: "the bloody strike in Chicago." This refers to the violent supression of the Haymarket riots (May 1–4, 1886).

Page 53: "he is in Mexico murdering Trotsky." After his expulsion from Norway, Leon Trotsky (1879–1940) moved his family outside Mexico City where he was murdered in 1940 by an alleged Stalinist agent he had taken into his confidence.

Page 57: In Greece the strength of a light bulb is measured in candle power, as well as watts.

Page 69: The reference to Liberty is to the painting of the French Revolution by Eugène Delacroix entitled *Liberty Leading the People*.

Page 69: "the painting of the Big Tower of Babel." This refers to Brueghel's painting.

Page 75: This poem with its imagery (Phrygian drum, thyrsus, lion, and maenads) reworks Euripides' *Bacchae*.

Tales of the Deep

Page 79: "What coincidence, sir, he said to me! What strange coincidence brings you to the house of the murderer." This foreboding epigraph is from Georgios Vizyenos's short story "Who was My Brother's Murderer" and is the only instance in which Mastoraki includes an explicit reference to another text. A translation of this tale can be found in *My Mother's Sin and Other Stories*, trans. William F. Wyatt Jr. (Hanover: University Press of New England, 1988).

Page 89: "My fair ones!" The adjective εύμορφα is an older form of όμορφα (beautiful) and sounds quaint to contemporary readers.

Page 91: "so they resemble you, torn to shreds, and you them, again, in pieces." The syntactical scrambling of subject and object in the original emphasizes the confusion that already distinguishes this poem. A literal translation would read: "in this way *they all* resemble *you* breaking *you* into pieces, and again *you* [resemble] *them* [breaking them] *all* [into] pieces."

Page 93: In this poem the word πανωπροίκι is used for "dowry," rather than the more usual προίκα, suggesting that a

Page 115: down payment or an extra amount of dowry was promised.

Page 115: "Uncle Jules." The reference is to the French author Jules Verne (1824–1905).

Page 119: In Greek the word for the person who commits suicide (αυτόχειρας) literally means "by one's own hand."

Page 143: "Arthur or Alphonse" addresses a plural reader, drawing on many possible intertexts such as the Arthurian romance, the *Poem of the Cid*, French romantic novels, and Edgar Allen Poe's *Narrative of Arthur Gordon Pym, of Nantucket*.

Hers

Page 153: "The past scrubbed with water and ashes." This line refers to the way women in Greece used to clean white clothes by rubbing ashes into the fabric.

Page 153: As in English, the main place that ίασπις και ίασμος (jasper and jasmine) are spatially opposed is in the dictionary.

Page 157: "Fair daylight." The line in the original is taken from the standard Greek translation of Shakespeare's *King Lear*, where Lear, struggling with madness, asks "Where have I been? Where am I? Fair daylight?" (4.6.49)

Page 171: "anathematic" (αναθηματικό). This term is used by archaeologists to describe an object on which a votive inscription or visual depiction of a tribute has been carved.

Page 249: In the Greek edition the line *"could it be someone else staring out?"* is mirrored on the right-hand page in the line from the next poem "Could it be someone else staring out?" creating the illusion that the page itself is a mirror.

Page 259: This is a reference to the writer Virginia Woolf (1882–1941, who committed suicide by drowning.

Page 281:   "She invoked her name." In Greek the same verb form (ἐπικαλέστηκε) is used for both the reflexive and middle sense. This sentence could also be translated "Her name was invoked."

FURTHER READING

Greek Women's Writing in Translation

Anagnostaki, Loula. 1984. "The City: A Trilogy of One-Act Plays." Translated by George Valamvanos and Kenneth MacKinnon. *Charioteer* 26:37–88.

Anghelaki-Rooke. 1975. *The Body is the Victory and the Defeat of Dreams*. Translated by Philip Ramp. San Francisco: Wire Press.

———. 1986. *Beings and Things on Their Own*. Translated by Jackie Wilcox (with author). Brockport, N.Y.: BOA Editions.

Barnstone, Aliki, and Willis Barnstone, eds. 1980. *A Book of Women Poets from Antiquity to Now*. New York: Schocken.

Dalven, Rae, ed. 1994. *Daughters of Sappho: Contemporary Greek Women Poets*. Foreword by Andonis Decavalles, and a preface by Karen Van Dyck. Rutherford: Fairleigh Dickinson University Press.

Dimoula, Kiki. 1996. *Lethe's Adolescence*. Translated by David Connolly. Minneapolis, Minn.: Nostos Books.

Douka, Maro.[1979] 1991. *Fool's Gold*. Translated by Roderick Beaton. Athens: Kedros.

Fakinou, Eugenia [1982] 1991. *Astradeni*. Translated by H. E. Criton. Athens: Kedros.

———. [1983] 1991. *The Seventh Garment*. Translated by Ed Emory. London: Serpent's Tail.

Fourtouni, Eleni, ed. 1978. *Contemporary Greek Women Poets*. New Haven, Conn.: Thelphini Press.

———. 1982. *Four Greek Women: Love Poems*. New Haven, Conn.: Thelphini Press.

———. 1986. *Greek Women in Resistence: Journals—Oral Histories*. New Haven, Conn.: Thelphini Press.

Friar, Kimon, ed. 1973. *Modern Greek Poetry: From Cavafis to Elytis*. With an introduction, an essay on translation, and notes. New York: Simon and Schuster.

———.1985. *Contemporary Greek Poetry*. With introduction, biographies, and notes. Athens:Ypourgio Politismou.

Galanaki, Rhea. 1996. *The Life of Ismail Ferik Pasha*. Translated by Kay Cicellis. London: Peter Owen.

Gogou, Katerina. 1983. *Three Cities Left*. Translated by Jack Hirschman. San Francisco: Night Horn Books.

Karapanou, Margarita. 1976. *Kassandra and the Wolf*. Translated by Nick Germanacos. New York: Harcourt Brace Jovanovich.

Leontis, Artemis, ed. 1997. *Greece: A Travellers' Literary Companion*. San Francisco: Whereabouts Press. Includes some short stories by women.

Liberaki, Margarita. 1959. *The Other Alexander*. Translated by Willis and Halle Tzalopoulou Barnstone. New York: Noonday Press.

———. [1946] 1995. *Three Summers*. Translated by Karen Van Dyck. Athens: Kedros.

Melissanthi. 1987. *Hailing the Ascending Morn: Selected Poems*. Translated and with an introduction by Maria Voelker-Kamarinea. Athens: Prosperos.

Moutzan-Martinengou, Elisavet. [1881] 1989. *My Story*. Translated by Helen Dendrinou Kolias. Athens: University of Georgia Press.

Siotis, Dinos, ed. (Summer) 1981. *The Coffeehouse: Contemporary Greek Arts and Letters* 10.

———. 1982. *Ten Women Poets of Greece*. Introduction by Katerina Anghelaki-Rooke. San Francisco: Wire Press.

Siotis, Dinos, and John Chioles, eds. 1979. *Twenty Contemporary Greek Poets*. San Francisco: Wire Press.

Sotiriou, Dido. 1991. *Farewell Anatolia*. Translated by Fred A. Reed. Athen: Kedros.

Valako, Eleni. 1971. *Geneaology*. Translated by Paul Merchant. Exeter: Rougemont Press.

———. 1982. "Selected Poems." Translated by Kimon Friar. *Journal of the Hellenic Diaspora* 9/4 (Winter): 28–43.

Zatelli, Zirana. 1985. "Birds." Translated by Kay Cicellis. *Translation* 14 (Spring) 28–37.

Zei, Alki. 1968. *Wildcat Under Glass*. Translated by Edward Fenton. New York: Holt, Rinehart and Winston. 1969. London: Gollancz.

———. 1972. *Petros' War*. Translated by Edward Fenton. New York: Dutton.

———. 1979. *The Sound of the Dragon's Feet*. Translated by Edward Fenton. New York: Dutton.

———. [1987] 1991. *Achilles' Fiancée*. Translated by Gail Holst-Warhaft. Athen: Kedros.

Relevant Criticism

Anastasopoulou, Maria. 1991. "Bildung, Awakening and Self/Redefinition in Greek Women Writers." *Modern Greek Studies Yearbook* 7:259–85.

———. 1997. "Feminist Discourse and Literary Representation in Turn-of-the-Century Greece: Kallirrhoë Siganou-Parren's 'The Book of Dawn'" *Journal of Modern Greek Studies* 15/1:1–28.

Anghelaki-Rooke, Katerina. 1983. "Sex Roles in Modern Greek Poetry." *Journal of Modern Greek Studies* 1/1:141–56.

Bohandy, Susan. 1994. "Defining the Self through the Body in Four Poems by Katerina Anghelaki-Rooke and Sylvia Plath." *Journal of Modern Greek Studies* 12/1:1–36.

Chioles, John. 1993. "Poetry and Politics: The Greek Cultural Dilemma." In *Ritual, Power, and the Body: Historical Perspectives on the Representation of Greek Women*, edited by C. Nadia Serematakis, 151–72. New York: Pella.

Coriolano-Lykourezos, Marina, ed. Forthcoming. *Babel Guide to Modern Greek Literature*. London: Babel Guides. Includes reviews of Greek women's literature.

Farinou-Malamatari, Georgia. 1988 "The Novel of Adolescence Written by a Woman: Margarita Limberaki." In *The Greek Novel: a.d. 1–1985*, edited by Roderick Beaton, 103–9. London: Croom Helm.

Faubion, James D. 1993. "The Works of Margharita Karapanou:

Literature as a Technology of Self-Formation." In *Modern Greek Lessons: A Primer in Historical Constructivism*, 184–212. Princeton: Princeton University Press.

Friar, Kimon. 1982. "Eleni Vakalo: Beyond Lyricism." *Journal of the Hellenic Disapora* 9/4 (Winter): 21–27

Kakavoulia, Maria. 1985. "Telling, Speaking, Naming in Melpo Axioti's *Would You Like to Dance, Maria?*" In *The Text and its Margins*, edited by Margaret Alexiou and Vassilis Lambropoulos, 123–56. New York: Pella.

Kolias, Helen Dendrinou. 1988. "Greek Women Poets and the Language of Silence." In *Translation Perspectives IV, Selected Papers, 1986–87*, 99–112. Binghamton, N.Y. National Resource Center for Translation and Interpretation.

Philippides, Dia M. L. 1990. *Checklist of English-Language Sources Useful in the Study (CENSUS) of Modern Greek Literature (1824–1987)*. New Haven, Conn.: Modern Greek Studies Association. The best source for checking whether an author has been translated.

Robinson, Christopher. 1984. "The Comparison of Greek and French Women Poets: Myrtiotissa, Maria Polydure, Anna de Noailles." *Journal of Modern Greek Studies.* 2/1:23–38.

———. 1996. "'Helen or Penelope?' Women Writers, Myth and the Problem of Gender Roles." In *Ancient Greek Myth in Modern Greek Poetry*, edited by Peter Mackridge, 109–20. London: Frank Cass.

Van Dyck, Karen. 1990. Introduction (as guest editor) and "The Sexual Politics of Babel." Translation Issue, *Journal of Modern Greek Studies* 8/2: 169–71, 173–82.

———. 1998. *Kassandra and the Censors: Greek Poetry since 1967*. Ithaca: Cornell University Press.

Karen Van Dyck directs the Program in Hellenic Studies at Columbia University where she teaches Modern Greek language and literature as well as courses in women's studies. The companion volume to this anthology is her critical study *Kassandra and the Censors: Greek Poetry since 1967* (Cornell University Press, 1998) in which she places the poetry of Rhea Galanaki, Maria Laina, and Jenny Mastoraki, among others, in its cultural context.

ABOUT THE POETS

Rhea Galanaki was born in Iraklion, Crete in 1947. She studied History and Archaeology at the University of Athens and now lives in Patras. She has published two volumes of poems, *Albeit Pleasing* (1975) and *Minerals* (1979), two poetic narratives, *The Cake* (1980) and *Where Does the Wolf Live?* (1982), a collection of short stories *Concentric Stories* (1986), two novels, *The Life of Ismail Ferik Pasha* (Spina nel Cuore) (1989) and *I Shall Sign my Name as Louis* (1993), and a collection of essays *King or Soldier* (1997). In 1987 she received the Nikos Kazantzakis Literary Award. *The Life of Ismail Ferik Pasha* is the first Greek novel to be included in the UNESCO collection of representative works (1994).

Maria Laina was born in Patras in 1947. She studied Law at the University of Athens. She has published six collections of poetry to date: *Coming of Age* (1968), *Beyond* (1970), *Change of Scene* (1972), *Punctuation Marks* (1979), *Hers* (1985), and *Rose Colored Fear* (1992), for which she received the National Literature Prize for Poetry (1994) and the City of Munich Literary Prize (1995). Her theatrical pieces are *The Clown* (1985), *Reality is Always Here* (1990) and *A Stolen Kiss* (1996). Her translations include the short stories of Katherine Mansfield and critical writings by Ezra Pound and T.S. Eliot.

Jenny Mastoraki was born in Athens in 1949 where she still lives. She studied Byzantine History and Literature at the University of Athens and has published five collections of poetry to date: *The Legend of St. Youth* (1971), *Tolls* (1972), *Kin* (1978), *Tales of the Deep* (1983), and *With a Crown of Light* (1989). She has translated extensively from American, Italian, German, and South American literature and criticism. In 1989 she received the Thornton Niven Wilder Prize from the Columbia University Translation Center in recognition of her contribution to the art of translation.

UNIVERSITY PRESS OF NEW ENGLAND publishes books under its
own imprint and is the publisher for Brandeis University Press, Dartmouth
College, Middlebury College Press, University of New Hampshire, Tufts
University, and Wesleyan University Press.

LIBRARY OF CONGRESS CATALOGING-IN-PUBLICATION DATA

The rehearsal of misunderstanding : three collections by contemporary
Greek women poets : bilingual edition / translated and with an introduction
by Karen Van Dyck.
    p.   cm.
Text in English and Greek.
Contents: The cake / by Rhea Galanaki. Tales of the deep / by Jenny
Mastoraki. Hers / by Maria Laina.
ISBN 0-8195-6327-7 (alk. paper). — ISBN 0-8195-6333-1 (pbk. : alk.
paper)
    1. Greek poetry, Modern—20th century—Translations into English.
    2. Greek poetry, Modern—Women authors—Translations into English.
    I. Van Dyck, Karen. II. Galanakē, Rea. Keik. English & Greek.
    III. Mastorakē, Tzenē, 1949- . Histories gia ta vathia. English & Greek.
    IV. Laina, Maria. Diko tēs. English & Greek.
PA5289.E6R44   1998
889'.1340809287—dc21   97–49979